BECAUSE *of* GRÁCIA

A FILM AND FAITH
CONVERSATION GUIDE

DEXTERITY

NASHVILLE

DEXTERITY

Dexterity, LLC 604 Magnolia Lane Nashville, TN 37211
Copyright © 2017

First edition: 2017 10 9 8 7 6 5 4 3 2 1

Printed in the United States of America.

ISBN: 978-1-947297-02-9 (trade paper) ISBN: 978-1-947297-03-6 (ebook)

Book design by Sarah Siegand Designs and Brian Kannard. Cover design by Trent Design, Inc.

Because of his great love for us, God, who is rich in mercy, made us alive with Christ even when we were dead in transgressions—it is by grace you have been saved.
Ephesians 2:4–5

TABLE OF CONTENTS

Theme III: Voicing Faith

CHRIS MASSOGLIA
Chase Morgan

Hello everyone! I play Chase Morgan in *Because of Grácia,* and I wanted to say thank you for checking out our student conversation guide. If you enjoyed the movie, I know you'll enjoy studying the themes within this book. For me, I've always felt certain topics should have been discussed more in my circles. I always had (and still have) questions regarding romantic relationships, how to relate to members of the opposite sex, and how to build my faith and follow Jesus better. I pray that as you go through these pages, your relationship with God will grow and you will be better equipped for life and for love.

As you work through this conversation guide, remember to listen to those who are older, wiser, and have a little more experience under their belts. As young people, we often want to find our own way; but I've been saved from so many bad decisions because I chose to listen to wisdom.

I also hope you can build closer relationships with the friends you discuss these important issues with. Don't be afraid to dive in and really share openly and honestly when you discuss each topic. Who knows the strength of the relationships that will be built out of this time?

Finally, I want to encourage you to rely on God's Word as your foundation. At the end of the day, we need to seek Jesus—through his words and his Spirit—to find the truth for every issue or life dilemma.

Be blessed and highly favored as you study on!

Peace,

Chris Massoglia

MORIAH PETERS
Grácia Davis

Hello, and welcome to a world of discussion about the film *Because of Grácia*. I play the role of Grácia Davis in the movie, a strong but complicated girl who's trying to live authentically. If you're reading this conversation guide, you're most likely trying to do something similar.

The practice of being guided through a thought process and challenged to ask difficult questions is something that has always helped me find a balanced perspective. As I recently read through the following pages you're about to encounter, I paused every so often to think carefully about what I was receiving. Give yourself the same space. As with any curriculum, the discussions here were designed to open your mind past the pages and off the screen.

We live in a culture where we are told quite loudly what to stand for and when to keep quiet. Challenging that worldly status quo happens to be one of my favorite things to do, and though I've gotten myself into trouble in the past, the biggest thing I've learned when it comes to the great question of "why?" is this: It's not only okay to ask, but it's good not to know all the answers. We weren't created for comfort, and we often meet God in the tension.

So, lean into the unknown. Take these conversations to the classroom and your friends and family and receive other people's points of view as valid and enriching. With this conversation guide and the background of the movie, and with Scripture beside you, you'll have a ton of content to consider. I'm so proud of you for wanting to dive further into the themes we presented in *Because of Grácia*.

Let me know sometime how you enjoy the journey!

XO,
Moriah Peters

INTRODUCTION

Dear Reader,

You hold in your hand a powerful resource for spiritual growth. The *Because of Grácia* conversation guide is an awesome way to take what you're learning when your whole group meets together and to set it in motion throughout your everyday life.

Just as with sports or music or academics or the arts, you need to "practice" your faith to see it grow. The basketball player shoots hoops after dinner. The guitarist jams with her friends whenever she can. What's the equivalent process for Christians (who may very well be basketball players and guitarists at the same time)? We'd like to suggest journeying through this book as one example of an answer.

Don't think of this book as one more piece of homework to do. You may indeed put this guide on your daily to-do list, but we hope you'll view it less like a duty and more like something you look forward to each day.

That's why we've designed this book for you to use with a friend. In the pages that follow, we call this person your "conversation partner." Ideally, the two of you will touch base for twenty minutes on a daily basis, five days a week: perhaps before or after school, at your house or your friend's house, at the park or café, or even over the phone, Skype, or FaceTime. That said, most activities in this book work best through face-to-face conversation.

Each paired session entry includes an introduction to the day's theme, scripture to read, questions to discuss, and activities to help explore the ideas further. There is space in this book to record your thoughts in writing, if you like doing that—but you and your partner may prefer to talk through it. The choice is yours.

When we made *Because of Grácia*, we imagined you enjoying it, learning from it, and applying its lessons to your everyday life. We pray this guide will assist you and encourage you along the way, both during your group sessions and your partnered conversations. By the end of your journey through this guide, we hope you will think of Chase, Grace, OB, and the other characters as friends.

We wish you a great time and much joyful discovery on this 45-day adventure in discipleship.

Chris Friesen and Michelle Simes

PRACTICING FRIENDSHIP

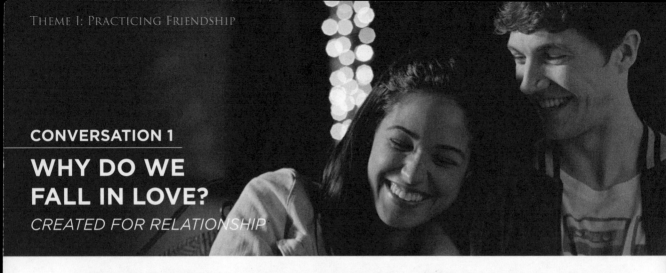

CONVERSATION 1

WHY DO WE FALL IN LOVE?

CREATED FOR RELATIONSHIP

GROUP SESSION

Is it a good thing that human beings fall in love with each other? Why is relationship, attraction, and romantic love such a tricky area of life? How could those relationships be easier? Today we look at Chase Morgan's awkward crush on a new student and the oldest male-female relationship known to humankind.

 **REEL to REAL**

1. Chase falling for Grace

- How can you tell Chase is falling for Grace? What effect is she having on him?

- Why are we drawn to certain people? Is it a simple thing or a complicated thing?

- Why is it so hard for Chase to take the initiative to get to know Grace? What is the "pressure" he's feeling? What is he afraid of?

2. The phone call

- Can you relate to Chase's experience in this situation? Is it true to life?

- Is awkwardness and nervousness with someone we're attracted to more of a guy thing or more a girl thing? Do girls show nervousness in different ways than guys do?

- What do we want most from someone we admire?

3. What came of it

- Do Chase and Grace feel the same way about each other?

- Why isn't Grace afraid to ask Chase to meet up somewhere?

- How is Chase feeling after the phone call?

ENGAGE THE WORD

After you examine Genesis 2:4–25 as a group, consider the questions below.

- Why isn't it good to be alone?

- Wasn't it enough for Adam to have God as a friend?

- What does it say about God that he recognizes Adam's need for companionship with someone similar to Adam?

- What do you think it means that woman was "taken out of man"?

- Does this story explain why we fall in love?

DAY 1:
LONGING FOR GOD
Week 1: WHY DO WE FALL IN LOVE?

In the movie clips at the first group session, we saw Chase Morgan meet a new classmate and have his world turned upside-down. "I can't stop thinking about her," he tells his favorite teacher, Mr. Brady.

Chase's nervousness illustrates the way men and women, guys and girls, long for each other in this world. It's not a flaw of creation that we have such a longing. Rather, it's a good feature that God purposely built into the very nature of things.

We also heard in the first group session how humanity's turning from God created a break that makes companionship between men and women—and all people—more difficult. We still need each other as we did at the start of creation, but now we also distrust each other and hide our true selves. Selfishness and sin have made us less able to meet others' needs and others less able to meet ours. Even worse, in our estrangement from God, we may begin to look to other human beings for ultimate fulfillment—not realizing our deepest relational need is actually for Someone divine.

What a mess! But many longing souls since Adam and Eve have realized the true nature of their need and reached for God first.

Read the Word 📖

Read through these verses from Psalm 63 twice with your conversation partner, taking turns. The first time through, read the text quietly sitting side by side. The second time, sit facing each other as far apart as the room will allow and read as loudly as necessary to be able to hear each other.

You, God, are my God, earnestly I seek you; I thirst for you, my whole being longs for you, in a dry and parched land where there is no water. I have seen you in the sanctuary and beheld your power and your glory. Because your love is better than life, my lips will glorify you. I will praise you as long as I live, and in your name I will lift up my hands. I will be fully satisfied as with the richest of foods; with singing lips my mouth will praise you. On my bed I remember you; I think of you through the watches of the night. Because you are my help, I sing in the shadow of your wings.
Psalm 63:1–8

Talk It Over 💬

Discuss the following questions with your conversation partner. If you like, write down your ideas as you go.

- What words and phrases in this psalm could apply to a human relationship?

- How is loving God similar to loving a human being?

- How is loving God different from loving a human being?

Listen Up 🎧

What is the most "romantic" worship song you've ever heard? In other words, what song expresses love for Jesus or God in a way that sounds the like the love between a man and a woman? Find a version of the song on YouTube and share the link with your conversation partner.

Think It Over

Is there any problem with expressing love to God and Jesus in this way? Are we confusing two different kinds of relationship? Or are we linking two kinds of relationship that are deeply linked in reality?

The more you read the Bible—a long love story about God and people—the more you may find the second answer to be true. The God who has created us for relationship often nudges us to consider our relationship with him through the lens of human love. Prophets like Zephaniah speak of God's loving delight in his people (Zephaniah 3:17). Jesus and the church are compared to husband and wife (Ephesians 5). Jesus's ultimate union with his people will be celebrated like a wedding banquet (Revelation 19).

Beginning a love relationship with God and satisfying our deepest relational need is one of the best steps we can take toward discovering fulfilling love relationships with one another. As Chase says later in the movie, "Jesus took this dead heart of nature and made it so much more alive."

Pray It Forward

Choose a sentence from Psalm 63 to use as a closing prayer for this first session with your conversation partner. Write the sentence down and carry it with you in your mind as a "background prayer" for the rest of the day.

DAY 2:
JUST GOTTA GET NEAR YOU
Week 1: WHY DO WE FALL IN LOVE?

When you're falling in love with someone, you want to be near them as much as possible. You find ways to make that happen. Remember Chase peering over the top of a book in the library or watching Grácia in class out of the corner of his eye? Maybe you arrange to be in that person's group, or sit next to that person on the bus, or whatever—just as long as you can be as physically close to them as possible. You also want that person to see and know and admire you in return.

This is how God expressed his love for human beings too. God's version of "falling in love" with us—though there was never a time he didn't love us—was to "fall" right down to earth in the flesh. When God came near us in Jesus, his Son, he got as close to human beings as possible. He became what we are so he could know everything about us and see the world through our eyes. At the same time, he gave us the opportunity to really know him. He poured all of himself into Jesus, putting his personality and character on display right before our eyes.

Read the Word

These sentences from the Bible describe how God's love brought him near us. Take turns reading them with your conversation partner.

For God so loved the world that he gave his one and only Son.
John 3:16

The Son is the radiance of God's glory and the exact representation of his being.
Hebrews 1:3

For in Christ all the fullness of the Deity lives in bodily form.
Colossians 2:9

For God was pleased to have all his fullness dwell in him, and through him to reconcile to himself all things.
Colossians 1:19–20

"If you really know me, you will know my Father as well. From now on, you do know him and have seen him. . . Anyone who has seen me has seen the Father."
John 14:7, 9

This is how God showed his love among us: He sent his one and only Son into the world that we might live through him.
1 John 4:9

Play It Over

Play a short game of charades based on these verses. The object is to get your partner to name the scripture you're thinking of by wordlessly acting out portion of the verse.

Talk It Over

Discuss the following questions with your conversation partner. If you like, write down your ideas as you go.

*   When you like somebody, how do you behave around them?

*   How do you try to "get yourself noticed"?

*   Do you think it's appropriate to say that God was "showing off" to humanity in Jesus? Why or why not?

*   What is something specific Jesus has demonstrated to you about what God is like?

Pose this question to a married adult you trust: "When you first started noticing your future husband or wife, was there anything special you did to get his or her attention?"

Pray It Forward 🙏

Dear God, thank you for your love that has reached so far without ever giving up. I ask you today to open my eyes and heart to know you more.

Love, _____

DAY 3:
CLOSER STILL
Week 1: WHY DO WE FALL IN LOVE?

Not only did God find a way to get near us in Jesus, but also he found a way to get inside us. Sometimes we talk about wanting to get inside someone's head. God wanted to get inside our hearts—that is, into our center, the innermost place of our thinking-feeling-loving-and-choosing.

At some time or another in your life, perhaps when you were a child, you may have heard about "inviting Jesus into your heart." You may even have done so. Where does that phrase come from? What does it really mean for Jesus to enter and take up residence in a person's heart?

Read the Word 📖

Listen to this prayer written by the apostle Paul. Choose one person to read and let the other person listen with their eyes closed. Then switch places and read it again.

For this reason I kneel before the Father, from whom every family in heaven and on earth derives its name. I pray that out of his glorious riches he may strengthen you with power through his Spirit in your inner being, so that Christ may dwell in your hearts through faith. And I pray that you, being rooted and established in love, may have power, together with all the Lord's holy people, to grasp how wide and long and high and deep is the love of Christ, and to know this love that surpasses knowledge—that you may be filled to the measure of all the fullness of God.
Ephesians 3:14–19

Talk It Over 💬

• When you invite Jesus to live in your heart, what does he do in there?

• Is there any particular word or phrase in this passage that surprises you? Which one?

Think It Over

When the New Testament talks about relationship with God through Jesus, it doesn't only mention him living in us. It also speaks of us living in him. In other words, our relationship with Jesus works in both directions. Being a Christian means that Christ is in us (Colossians 1:27), and it is also means we are in Christ (2 Corinthians 5:17).

Dream it Up 🎨

Get two sheets of paper and some pens. Imagine you are an artist and you have traveled to a place where people speak and write a language you don't know. You have been asked to paint them a picture of these verses from Ephesians. Make a quick, rough plan for your painting on the paper you have. Set a timer for 3–5 minutes while both you and your conversation partner take a shot at it. Don't worry how "good" it looks: Remember, it's just a plan. When you're done, show each other your sketches and compare them with the scripture passage. (If you're on the phone and can't see your partner, hang on to your plan until you see each other next.)

One time, Jesus wrapped it all together. He said: "On that day you will realize that I am in my Father, and you are in me, and I am in you" (John 14:20).

- If you are a Christian, which way of thinking about it makes more sense to you: you living in Christ, or Christ living in you?

- If you are not a Christian, what questions do you have about living with Christ?

When Jesus lives inside us, there is a new connection between our hearts and his. The Holy Spirit, the presence of Jesus within us, changes our hearts to be like his, makes our hearts feel what his does, and helps us relate to God in the same way Jesus does—as a beloved child.

As Chase says in his spoken-word poem to his class, "It's this beautiful silver piano chord between me and my Lord, and it's making the most beautiful melody that the world has ever heard. And it's a melody that Jesus offers the entire world."

Pray It Forward

If you have never done so, you could ask Jesus today, even right now, to make his home in your heart.

DAY 4:
RELATIONSHIP IS WHO GOD IS
Week 1: WHY DO WE FALL IN LOVE?

God did not create the world for some unknown reason and then decide he might as well be loving toward it. God pursues relationship with his creation because that is the essence of who he is. Considering God's oneness as Father, Son, and Holy Spirit, we might even say that God is relationship.

Does that sound weird? It shouldn't. It's only a minor paraphrase of the language of the Bible itself, which says, "God is love." Because we are made in God's image, we too pursue relationship and love.

The book of 1 John makes this point powerfully. John says that because of God's essential relational character, we actually come to know him by loving others. else. John says that because of God's essential relational character, we actually come to know him by loving others.

Read the Word
Read these verses out loud with your conversation partner:

Dear friends, let us love one another, for love comes from God. Everyone who loves has been born of God and knows God. Whoever does not love does not know God, because God is love.
1 John 4:7–8

Dear friends, since God so loved us, we also ought to love one another. No one has ever seen God; but if we love one another, God lives in us and his love is made complete in us.
1 John 4:11–12

God is love. Whoever lives in love lives in God, and God in them.
1 John 4:16

We love because he first loved us.
1 John 4:19

Relationship is so important—and not only the special relationship between male and female, but all kinds of relationship, including love for friends, family, church, and world.

Talk It Over 💬

- What statement do you find most remarkable in the verses from 1 John?

- Do John's words stir up any questions for you?

- How might our Christian lives and communities be different if we took these words completely seriously?

Try It Out ✔

Back in Genesis, God said it wasn't good for his image-bearer to be alone. Keep watch this week for someone at your school or elsewhere who is alone on a regular basis. Start talking to that person.

Pray It Forward 🙏

God, here is an area of my life where I probably have more to learn about "loving one another":

As I learn to love more, help me to know you as well. In Jesus's name, amen.

MEME-orize It 🖼

Choose one phrase or sentence from these verses and use it as a caption for an image you find. Share your resulting meme with your conversation partner.

DAY 5:
GOD CARES HOW WE RELATE
Week 1: WHY DO WE FALL IN LOVE?

What we've been learning about the importance of love and relationship to God leads to a warning: If we begin to harm others in relationships, we immediately begin to distance ourselves from God. That's what Cain found out when he killed his brother Abel, which is documented in Genesis 4.

Read the Word
Here's how the writer of 1 John expresses the problem. Read the passage aloud twice.

Whoever claims to love God yet hates a brother or sister is a liar. For whoever does not love their brother and sister, whom they have seen, cannot love God, whom they have not seen. And he has given us this command: Anyone who loves God must also love their brother and sister.
1 John 4:20–21

Talk It Over

- What other words could you substitute into this passage in place of the words *brother* and *sister*? Think of at least three and write them here.

Read the Word

And here's how Jesus expresses it:

"Therefore, if you are offering your gift at the altar and there remember that your brother or sister has something against you, leave your gift there in front of the altar. First go and be reconciled to them; then come and offer your gift."
Matthew 5:23–24

Talk It Over

- What is Jesus saying about God?

- Why does God care so much about our relationships with each other?

Think It Over

There are some relationship loose ends in *Because of Grácia.* At the end of the film, a few people have broken relationships with one another (for example, Bobbi and Jesse, Chase and Josie). Can anything be done to repair those situations?

Pray It Forward

Pray for someone in your life whom you might have hard feelings toward or who might have hard feelings toward you. Ask God to make a way for reconciliation to take place.

CONVERSATION 2

WHAT ABOUT OUR BODIES?

GOD'S DESIGN FOR SEXUALITY

GROUP SESSION

We've learned that we're made for relationship, but we also know that we exist in physical bodies that often seem to have minds of their own. How do you deal with such powerful forces this side of marriage? Today we'll take a look at a young couple that makes some mistakes in this area and hear about the fresh start that is available even after making such mistakes.

 **REEL to REAL**

1. Bobbi and Jesse home alone

- What do you find most true-to-life about this scene?

- Why are Christians supposed to reserve sex for marriage anyway?

- Jesse says, "I just kinda do what comes natural." Is there any problem with that as a standard for life and relationships?

- Jesse also says a couple things that draw Bobbi back into making out: 1) he's unbelievably attracted to the most beautiful woman he knows; and 2) "You're making me believe, Bobbi. You're making me believe." Why do his words have that effect on her?

2. At the tracks and afterward

- "Oh God, what am I doing?" Bobbi says. Do you think young people plan to get into situations like this, or do they get there without really knowing where they're going?

- "I don't want you to feel any pressure. I just want you to know that I love you," Jesse says. Is he pressuring her or not?

- Imagine Bobbi's inner monologue as she sits in the car wondering what to do. What is she thinking?

- What are some words to describe the mood as Jesse drives Bobbi home and says goodnight? Why are they feeling this way?

- Twice in these scenes, Jesse tells Bobbi that he loves her. Love can mean many different things. What is Jesse trying to say?

3. Grace tells her story

- How did Grace end up in a negative relationship at her previous school?

- Did your opinion of Grace change once you heard her story? If so, in what way?

- Is it possible to live a lifestyle of purity again after one has done what Grace did? How does that happen?

- Grace says of God: "He loves Bobbi, he loves me, no matter what we've done." Do you believe that?

ENGAGE THE WORD

After your leader reads the account in John 8:1–11 of the woman caught in adultery, consider the following questions.

- Imagine being present at this scene. Which character do you most identify with?

- Does Jesus care that this woman committed adultery?

- In what way does he give her a fresh start in life?

- Have you ever experienced this kind of a fresh start in life? Do you need to experience it now?

CARRY IT OUT

With your small group, read through 1 Corinthians 6:18–20 and dream up a way to set it to music. You might create a rap that quotes words of the text, or you might choose another popular song that you know and change the words to incorporate some scripture. Though the subject matter is profound, have some fun with it.

DAY 1:
THE GOOD GIFT OF SEX
Week 2: WHAT ABOUT OUR BODIES?

Do you ever think of God as an all-knowing, all-seeing deity who is just waiting for you to mess up? Do you imagine him as a solitary figure watching the people on earth, keeping tabs on their every move, setting traps for them, and resenting their enjoyment of life?

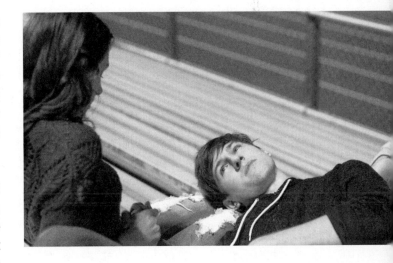

If you do, that is so unfair to God! That's just how the serpent in the garden of Eden wanted Eve to think of God (Genesis 3). But if God had a resentful attitude toward human beings and sex, why would he have created male and female in the first place? In that case, he never would have presented Eve to Adam; and he never would have told them to "be fruitful and increase in number" (Genesis 1:28).

It's important to remember that all true pleasure in the world comes from God, who "richly provides us with everything for our enjoyment" (1 Timothy 6:17). Scripture's overall view of the Creator of the world is not as a stingy dictator but as a generous father interested in our joy.

Read the Word

Read these Bible texts out loud one by one.

God saw all that he had made, and it was very good.
Genesis 1:31

Every good and perfect gift is from above, coming down from the Father of the heavenly lights, who does not change like shifting shadows.
James 1:17

How priceless is your unfailing love, O God! People take refuge in the shadow of your wings. They feast on the abundance of your house; you give them drink from your river of delights. For with you is the fountain of life; in your light we see light.
Psalm 36:7–9

"The thief comes only to steal and kill and destroy; I have come that they may have life, and have it to the full."
John 10:10

Take delight in the Lord, and he will give you the desires of your heart.
Psalm 37:4

Think It Over

These scriptures are not saying that God gives us every single thing we desire. They don't say that God is a weak parent, anxious to keep his demanding children satisfied. Instead, they say that God gives us the best—for our best.

God does not resent the sexual enjoyment human beings experience. The inclusion of Song of Songs in the Bible—a book that doesn't even mention God by name—should more than convince us of that fact. At the same time, God intends this powerful gift for a particular use: the expression and reinforcement of the covenant bond of marriage, where husband and wife become "one flesh" (Genesis 2:24) both spiritually and emotionally and in terms of new lives that they may create.

Talk It Over

- When Bobbi and Jesse are cuddling on the couch early on in the movie, she says to him, "As a Christian I'm not supposed to. . . have sex." Does putting it this way promote an unfair view of God?

- Even though Bobbi is pretty distracted in that moment, how might she have expressed the need for them to slow down in a way that would have honored the true biblical view of pleasure and sex?

- What's your favorite phrase in the verses you read today?

Pray It Forward
Thank God for some good and perfect gifts he has given you.

Then pray: *Abba Father, teach me above all to delight myself in you.*

DAY 2:
THE GOOD GIFT OF LAW
Week 2: WHAT ABOUT OUR BODIES?

Anything good can become harmful when taken outside of God's design. Take eating, for example. Like sex, it's another pleasurable body action connected both to the sustenance of life and the strengthening of relationship. Eating is wonderful!

And yet eating can go wrong, as demonstrated by gluttony, addiction, and eating disorders. If you consider the kinds of diseases prevalent in our culture, eating can actually kill us.

That's why God's detailed laws about sexuality for the people of Israel weren't arbitrary or cruel. God gave them laws because he loved them. He didn't want to see his good gift of sex turned to envy and theft, shame and sickness, violence and death. The Bible provides plenty of examples of that kind of thing taking place. (Think of the results of King David's affair with Bathsheba, for instance.) Since sex is such a powerful good, to distort it does powerful harm.

Read the Word 📖

God provides law to make life better: "so that you may live long in the land the Lord your God is giving you" (Exodus 20:12). Biblical law comes from a God who "delights in the well-being" of his servants (Psalm 35:27)—including their sexual well-being. That's why the servants can pray, trustingly, "Direct me in the path of your commands, for there I find delight" (Psalm 119:35). Even people who don't like a certain law, not understanding the reason for it, can still benefit from its protection.

You shall not commit adultery.
Exodus 20:14

Kind of an odd word, this *adultery* thing. We tend to think of it as cheating on a spouse—something *adults* do—so what's the relevance to young people? Or is it possible that all sex outside of marriage—even sex between two unmarried people—falls into the same category?

Think It Over

Well, we could debate that one all day. And people do. But the problem with a legal orientation to life is that it doesn't go far enough. We could argue endlessly about the precise meaning of the law, looking for as many loopholes as possible.

That's the place Bobbi and Jesse find themselves one evening. "I don't see anyone having sex here," Jesse says on the couch in her living room. Indeed, their clothes are on, and they are not having intercourse. They're within the letter of the law, right?

But the point is, where are they going? Can they go in that direction and still honor the heart of God's design for sexuality? The answer is no—they can't.

A Christian respects law but reaches even higher. That's the pattern we learn from Jesus in the Sermon on the Mount, in which he said that even just looking lustfully at another person is committing adultery in your heart (Matthew 5:28). Jesus points to the deeper intention of the law, not the mere letter of it. And he gives his Spirit to those who follow him, empowering them to to live by that high standard. The patience and self-control produced in us by the Spirit of Jesus (Galatians 5:22–23) helps us recognize that sex before marriage does not embrace God's good intention for relationship.

Ask A Mentor

With your conversation partner or on your own, invite a trusted married adult to meet you for coffee or converse on FaceTime or Skype. Ask them, "Does sex before marriage fit with God's design?" If it feels awkward to do this, tell them you're asking as an assignment from the *Because of Grácia* conversation guide.

Talk It Over 🗩

- What do you think about all this? Do you agree? If you could ask Jesus one question on the subject, what would you ask?

Pray It Forward 🙏

God of love and truth, light and joy, give me the power to live within your dazzling intentions for me. Direct me in the path of your commands, for there I find delight!

DAY 3:
THE MUSIC OF OUR BODIES
Week 2: WHAT ABOUT OUR BODIES?

Law often uses the language of "do not" as a way of simplifying life. (Do not lie, do not steal, do not murder . . . you catch the drift.) We know we're not supposed to have sex as unmarried people. So what are we supposed to do with these complicated, beautiful, risky bodies God has given us?

Here's an idea.

Think of your body as a musical instrument. What kind of music does it play? What lyrics go along with the music? Is the tune always the same, or does it change in different circumstances? Who is the composer of the music, and who is the conductor?

Read the Word

The apostle Paul had a lot to say about dealing with the impulses of our bodies. In the following passage he speaks of our bodies as "instruments." That has the general meaning of "tools," but let's keep the musical instrument metaphor going.

Each conversation partner can read the passage out loud once to the other.

Count yourselves dead to sin but alive to God in Christ Jesus. Therefore do not let sin reign in your mortal body so that you obey its evil desires. Do not offer any part of yourself to sin as an instrument of wickedness, but rather offer yourselves to God as those who have been brought from death to life; and offer every part of yourself to him as an instrument of righteousness.
Romans 6:11–13

Think It Over

There are some weighty words in this passage, especially *righteousness* and *sin*. What are these things?

Let's understand sin as anything that breaks the good purpose of God—anything that steals, kills, and destroys. And let's understand righteousness as everything that fulfills and expresses the good purpose of God—everything pure, lovely, noble, excellent, and beautiful.

Counting yourself dead to sin would mean saying to sin, "I don't listen to you anymore. You have no more control over me. You might as well consider me dead, for all the obedience you're going to get from me. I'm not your slave." From a musical point of view, you would be saying, "From now on, sin, I won't be playing your song."

Offering yourself to God, on the other hand, would mean saying, "Here I am, Lord. Take all of me—heart, mind, and body. Tune me up and position me in your symphony of creation. Every note will praise you."

God is ready to use your physical body for his good purposes in your life and the world, so offer it to him on a daily basis—sexual parts and all. We are not asking God to extinguish the sexual parts of ourselves, even if they seem troublesome. Instead, we are presenting those parts, desires, appetites, and needs to God *alive*— as a living sacrifice, not a dead one (Romans 12:1)—so that God may create something beautiful with them in his good time.

Talk It Over 💬

- What's your favorite style of music? If that music had no words at all, how would someone from another culture interpret it?

- What "music" do you want to present to the world with your body? What do you want that music to say?

Try It Out ✔

Do something healthy and energetic with your body today. Ride a bike, go swimming, spend some time outside, shoot some hoops, play guitar like Grácia, skateboard like Chase, rake someone's leaves, carry something for someone… The possibilities are endless!

Pray It Forward 🙏

During a time when David was really suffering, he said to God, "All my longings lie open before you" (Psalm 38:9). Repeat these words to God for yourself today, bearing in mind your sexual longings too.

DAY 4:
THERE'S MORE TO IT THAN YOU THINK
Week 2: WHAT ABOUT OUR BODIES?

In a way, experimentation like Bobbi and Jesse's is a bit like trying to drive on an urban highway before earning a license. Yes, they might know how to start the car and put it in gear, but can they control it safely from that point? They might not be as ready to drive as they think.

Similar to driving a car, sexuality has an established framework of readiness and a safe context in which the necessary skills can grow. Within that framework, sex can be fully explored and honored, fully disciplined and delighted in, and fully integrated with all other aspects of loving companionship. That framework, from a Christian perspective, is marriage.

A marriage covenant is your spiritual driver's license for sexual discovery. There's no learner's license, no practice period, no road test—just a preliminary study of the rules of the road and a lifelong commitment in the sight of God and a supportive community. Married people make many mistakes and hurt each other sometimes, but by and large, they'll be just fine with love, joy, peace, patience, kindness, goodness, faithfulness, gentleness, and self-control guiding them.

Read the Word 📖

Here is some scripture to go with these ideas.

When I was a child, I talked like a child, I thought like a child, I reasoned like a child. When I became a man, I put the ways of childhood behind me. For now we see only a reflection as in a mirror; then we shall see face to face. Now I know in part; then I shall know fully, even as I am fully known.
1 Corinthians 13:11–12

Paul is talking about spiritual maturity here, but what he says applies to other kinds of maturity as well, including sexual maturity. In another passage, he made an important analogy between those different but parallel relationships. (Check out Ephesians 5:25–33.)

Talk It Over 💬

• Marriage may be a long ways away for you yet. Do you think about it much?

• What would you say are the main reasons some young people start "driving without a license"— metaphorically speaking?

Pray It Forward 🙏

Freestyle day. Write your own prayer.

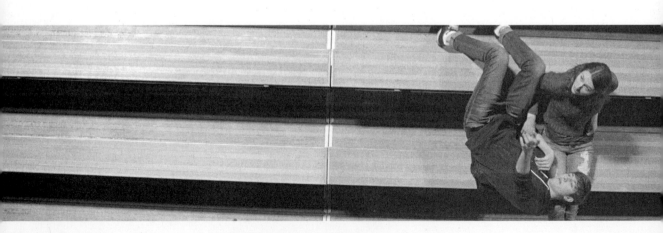

DAY 5:
WE WAIT FOR IT PATIENTLY
Week 2: WHAT ABOUT OUR BODIES?

If you've watched *Because of Grácia* to the final scene, you know where the story of Chase and Grácia leads. And you know that the new story of Chase and Grácia, which begins with a kiss at that point, will be all the sweeter for the waiting.

Going back to Eden for a moment, we could say that the real problem of eating from the forbidden tree was that Adam and Eve seized fruit on their own timeline rather than on God's. They took a shortcut in their impatience to be like him. But we realize from the rest of Scripture that it was always God's intention for us to be like him—just not in this sudden, grasping way.

We honor God, the giver of sexual love, by waiting until marriage to enjoy it. At that time, it can be fully celebrated in the context it's intended for.

Read the Word 📖

Christians waiting with hope for the "renewal of all things" (Matthew 19:28) know something about patient expectation. What if we tapped into this knowledge and applied it to the realm of relationship and sexuality?

Here are some biblical words that speak of our longing for the time when Jesus will close the present age and make all things new. Just as we've done before, we might steer these words a little outside their intended subject area and apply them imaginatively to the theme of patiently delayed sexuality.
Read the passage slowly with your conversation partner.

The creation waits in eager expectation for the children of God to be revealed. For the creation was subjected to frustration, not by its own choice, but by the will of the one who subjected it, in hope that the creation itself will be liberated from its bondage to decay and brought into the freedom and glory of the children of God.

We know that the whole creation has been groaning as in the pains of childbirth right up to the present time. Not only so, but we ourselves, who have the firstfruits of the Spirit, groan inwardly as we wait eagerly for our adoption to sonship, the redemption of our bodies. For in this hope we were saved. But hope that is seen is no hope at all. Who hopes for what they already have? But if we hope for what we do not yet have, we wait for it patiently.
Romans 8:19–25

Talk It Over 💬

- Which phrase in this passage do you find the strangest? Which do you find most encouraging?

- Name three things you are waiting for in your life right now.

- How do you find the patience to wait for them?

Listen Up 🎧

Listen to "White Boots" by Jamie Grace on YouTube for an upbeat portrayal of waiting patiently for marriage.

Try It Out ✔

Try some "waiting practice." Skip a meal that you would normally eat, and talk and sing to God during that time instead. Every time you feel hungry between then and your next meal, silently thank God for the good things he has planned for your future.

Pray It Forward 🙏

Take a moment to speak simple prayers of blessing, support, and encouragement for one another, knowing that the Spirit groans along with you, beyond what words can express (Romans 8:26).

CONVERSATION 3

HOW DO YOU GROW IN TRUE FRIENDSHIP?
HEALTHY DATING 101

GROUP SESSION

Christians need to be experts at the kind of love 1 Corinthians describes: patient, kind, humble, generous, protecting, forgiving, and more. Can we practice such values in friendship in a way that can lead to awesome, pure, joyful relationships? Today we watch a good example, and a not-so-good example, and talk about thinking differently when it comes to dating. Our culture may have its own way, but God's way rises above and beyond that of our culture and world.

 **REEL to REAL**

1. Chase and Grace's first date

- What's going on in this scene?

- Why does this situation begin so awkwardly for Chase? How does it get easier for him?

- Did you pick up any specific ideas on how to grow true friendship?

2. Bobbi and Jesse at the bleachers

- How is this conversation different from the last one we saw?

- When a young couple spends a lot of time exploring their physical attraction to one another, what might happen to other aspects of the relationship?

- Did you pick up any specific ideas on how to grow true friendship?

3. **Chase and Grace in her back yard**

- What was the problem with Grace's last dating relationship?

- What's your opinion of Chase and Grace's physical expressions of affection here: too much, not enough, or just right? What does the hand-holding and hug communicate?

- Which pattern of relationship do you see more of at your school: Chase and Grace's or Bobbi and Jesse's? How about in popular music, television, and movies?

HOW TO PLAY
DOUBLE DOUBLE

In a small group, play this hand game with a partner. See if you improve with some practice, then see if you can master it with another partner.

Chant the words and perform the actions at the same time, gradually getting faster as you go.

Actions

- *double:* bumping the soft sides of your fists with your partner's as though pounding on a door

- *this:* clapping your palms against your partner's

- *that:* clapping the backs of your palms against your partner's

Chant
double double this this
double double that that
double this double that
double double this that

ENGAGE THE WORD

After members of your group read Romans 11:33–12:2 aloud, consider the follow
questions.

- How do these words of the apostle Paul relate, either directly or indirectly, to th
  themes of friendship, love, and dating?

- What is "the pattern of this world" for relationships between guys and girls?

- What could it mean to "not conform to the pattern of this world" in this area of li

PAIRED SESSIONS

DAY 1:
SO THAT YOU MAY PRAY
Week 3: HOW DO YOU GROW IN TRUE FRIENDSHIP?

At their island fireplace, Grácia describes to Chase and OB how she got involved with the partying crowd at her last school. She says she started out thinking she could witness to them as their designated driver but soon found herself caught up in their pattern of life: drinking on weekends, dating without discernment, and losing sensitivity to God.

Imagining her to be "perfect" ("You're so—together," says OB), the guys are surprised to hear Grácia's story. Since they don't run with the in-crowd themselves, they may have underestimated the character-shaping power a peer group can have.

What should Christian young people do in this time and place? Should they keep separate from non-Christians to protect their character from bad influence? If they do, they have no opportunity to shine a light. Should they immerse themselves in the world like the apostle Paul did, becoming "all things to all people" (1 Corinthians 9:22)? If they do so without the training of someone like Paul, they risk losing themselves in the same way Grace did, especially if they try to go it alone.

In the last group session, we reflected on the words of Romans 12:2: "Do not conform to the pattern of this world, but be transformed by the renewing of your mind." This challenges us to present our minds to God for transformation, so as to be able to live out a new pattern in the world. Refusing to conform is not about being better than others, but about protecting our spiritual senses and maintaining the ability to hear and know and reach out to the One who loves us most.

Read the Word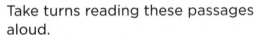

Take turns reading these passages aloud.

So I tell you this, and insist on it in the Lord, that you must no longer live as the Gentiles do, in the futility of their thinking. They are darkened in their understanding and separated from the life of God because of the ignorance that is in them due to the hardening of their hearts. Having lost all sensitivity, they have given themselves over to sensuality so as to indulge in every kind of impurity, and they are full of greed. That, however, is not the way of life you learned.
Ephesians 4:17–20

For you have spent enough time in the past doing what pagans choose to do—living in debauchery, lust, drunkenness, orgies, carousing and detestable idolatry. They are surprised that you do not join them in their reckless, wild living, and they heap abuse on you. But they will have to give account to him who is ready to judge the living and the dead.
1 Peter 4:3–5

Talk It Over 🗨

- Think of what it feels like to burn your tongue. (For some time afterward, you can't taste anything anymore.) Which of today's two passages would you say presents a spiritual equivalent of "burning your tongue"?

- Can you relate to these words: "They are surprised that you do not join them in their reckless, wild living, and they heap abuse on you"? Give a specific example from your experience.

- Why be clear-minded and self-controlled?

- What does any of this have to do with healthy dating and true friendship?

Play It Over

Find a heavy rap or hip-hop beat online, or get your conversation partner to beatbox one for you. Then read the two passages again with in-your-face flair.

Pray It Forward 🙏

Jesus prayed to God for his disciples before his arrest and crucifixion: "They are not of the world any more than I am of the world. My prayer is not that you take them out of the world but that you protect them from the evil one" (John 17:14–15).

Rewrite this prayer in your own words.

DAY 2:
BELIEVING TOGETHER
Week 3: HOW DO YOU GROW IN TRUE FRIENDSHIP?

"Jess, I'm a Christian," says Bobbi.

"I know," he replies, emphasizing his willingness to tolerate her personal preferences. He continues stroking her hair and neck.

"So you don't feel any guilt?" she asks a few moments later, curious about a state of mind so different from her own.

"Guilt would probably not describe how I'm feeling right now." Jesse goes on tell her she's the most beautiful woman he knows. When he confirms it with, "Honest to God," she's skeptical.

"I thought you didn't believe in God."

"Well you're making me believe, Bobbi. You're making me believe."

An exchange like this helps us predict the troubles approaching this young couple. It's the same kind of situation Grácia was in with the California boyfriend who didn't share her Christian faith.

A contrary spiritual outlook is nothing to mess around with in the area of love and dating. Faith is the deepest part of who we are and the most important compatibility factor we have to look for in a potential boyfriend, girlfriend, or marriage partner.

Does that mean all dating has to lead to marriage? Not at all. But there's little reason to date someone if marriage with them would be absolutely out of the question. Regardless of how distantly into the future we envision ourselves with a particular boyfriend or girlfriend, the kinds of lifestyle and activity decisions we have to make while dating must be made in cooperation with a person who looks at the meaning of life, and the Master of life, in the same way we do.

Read the Word 📖
2 Corinthians puts this forcefully.

Do not be yoked together with un-believers. For what do righteousness and wickedness have in common? Or what fellowship can light have with darkness? What harmony is there between Christ and Belial [a name for the devil]? Or what does a believer have in common with an unbeliever? What agreement is there between the temple of God and idols? For we are the temple of the living God. As God has said: "I will live with them and walk among them, and I will be their God, and they will be my people."
2 Corinthians 6:14–16

What does it mean to be "yoked"? The image is of two oxen working together to pull a load, joined at the shoulders by a carved wooden brace that lets them exert force side by side. A yoke is a metaphor for any partnership—and the strongest partnership we know of is marriage, right?

The instruction given to the Corinthian church about partnerships is pretty blunt. And for the most part, when it comes to marriage, Christians have obeyed it.

Should the instruction apply to dating too, in that case?

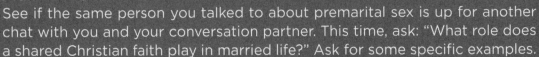

Ask A Mentor ❓
See if the same person you talked to about premarital sex is up for another chat with you and your conversation partner. This time, ask: "What role does a shared Christian faith play in married life?" Ask for some specific examples.

Talk It Over

- What does it mean to date someone? Does it always mean that you consider them your "girlfriend" or "boyfriend"?

- What's the point of having this kind of relationship anyway?

- Jonah says of his big sister, Grácia, that she wants to marry her best friend. What would that approach suggest about whom a person dates?

- If you had to rank the following possible "purposes of dating," what order would you put them in, from most to least important?
  - fun and recreation
  - learning how to relate to the opposite sex
  - emotional support
  - spiritual friendship
  - social status and popularity
  - discernment of a future marriage partner
  - help with homework
  - physical attraction

Pray It Forward

If there is someone you are attracted to these days, pray for that person's faith to grow. And pray for your own faith, that you might one day become a strong spiritual partner for another Christian. If there is no one you are interested in, tell God that you believe he has this area of your life entirely under control.

DAY 3:
PRACTICING "FRIENDSHIP FIRST"
Week 3: HOW DO YOU GROW IN TRUE FRIENDSHIP?

So you've found a special someone. You figure you may even want to marry them someday, although you're not too worried about that yet since you're still in high school. You already believe that sex is a good gift to save for marriage. Like Grace and Chase, you've decided to set yourself on a chaste pathway of "friendship first," so that if you do marry this person one day, you'll already have a solid foundation for a shared life.

Now, how do you go about putting this intention into practice in everyday life? How do you safeguard the tiny growing seedling of pure relationship?

Allow us to offer some practical suggestions.

1) *Meet the family.* Just as Grace does on her first get-together with Chase, involve your families from the very start. Meeting someone's family is a really important way of getting to know that person. Our families can also give us a clear-eyed perspective on any special friendship we're developing. It's significant that Pastor Ryan refers to Jesse as "that kid" during the crisis in their living room. It shows he never really got a chance to know Jesse.

2) *Spend time together with others.* Grace takes the initiative to convene a unique friendship circle on her backyard island most weekends. Even if OB protests that he is a "third wheel," his presence is crucial. Their togetherness focuses Chase and Grace on shared meaning rather than on the "what do we do now?" of frequent solitude. Bobbi and Jesse would have benefited from a few good friends to spend time with together.

3) *Ask good questions and give good answers.* Healthy friendship thrives on detailed communication. (One day, healthy marriage will depend on the very same thing, so you might as well practice it now.) That means posing and answering questions like, "Whatcha thinking?" and "How did you feel about that?" and "Do you see it the same way?" Really, it's about engaging in the nitty-gritty of discipleship together.

4) *Contain the physical.* When we begin to explore physical knowledge of someone else, it can quickly overwhelm social, emotional, intellectual, and spiritual dimensions of the relationship. When you start playing again and again with the power of the body, what need is there for conversation anymore? We see this happen with Bobbi and Jesse, even though she tries to steer it back for a while. Rules of thumb for this area? Well, there are commonsense guidelines like hands-off for areas of the body usually covered by a bathing suit. But even more important than rule-based boundaries is that we examine our underlying intentions and our general use of time. Is our degree of physical contact regularly awakening desires that can't be satisfied? That would be a sign that a more profound "rule" is needed.

Read the Word 📖

Here's a biblical encouragement on the last point.

Follow God's example, therefore, as dearly loved children and walk in the way of love, just as Christ loved us and gave himself up for us as a fragrant offering and sacrifice to God. But among you there must not be even a hint of sexual immorality, or of any kind of impurity, or of greed, because these are improper for God's holy people.
Ephesians 5:1-3

Pray It Forward 🙏

If you are in a relationship, or have been in a relationship, and if there is any area of pure and true friendship in which you have failed, know that you can lift up your failure to God, accept his forgiveness, and receive the power to turn things around and live in a new way. Take this promise to heart: "If we confess our sins, he is faithful and just and will forgive us our sins and purify us from all unrighteousness" (1 John 1:9).

God is ready to listen whenever you're ready to talk. If that is now, take the time to do so.

Talk It Over 💬

• Which of the four suggestions have you already experienced and put into practice?

• Which have you not?

DAY 4:
TELLING THE TRUTH
Week 3: HOW DO YOU GROW IN TRUE FRIENDSHIP?

To his credit, Jesse tries to speak truth to Bobbi in the way he knows how. "I had a really good time tonight," he says. And later, "I love you"—even if what he really means by that is something more like, "I'm sorry if you're upset, and I hope things are going to be okay between us."

But the kind of truth we want to talk about now is larger than personal experience. It's not so much *your* truth or *his* truth or *her* truth, but *the* truth.

One person might say to another, "I admire your physical being. I would like to possess it for myself. I want to experience pleasure with you. And I want you to want me, too." People send these kinds of messages with their bodies, words, and touches all the time, even with the way they dress and carry themselves. They tell a particular truth about themselves and their intentions. But the challenge for Christian practitioners of true friendship and holy dating is to learn to tell the whole truth—God's truth for relationship—to one another with their bodies.

Take the holding of another person's hand, for example. The way Chase and Grácia do this at a special moment in the film says, "I consider you a close friend. I trust you and believe in you. I want to support you and walk with you." Chase actually gives voice to these things verbally a moment beforehand: "I respect and admire you, Grácia, and your friendship means the world to me." And Grácia gives voice to it just before Chase leaves when she hugs him and says, "I'm so grateful for you, Chase."

They have spoken simple truth to one another. They have not reached beyond their current reality and said with their bodies, "We are committed to one another forever," or "We have created a permanent home and covenant in which children can safely grow." They aren't at that place yet. The sexual body language that would communicate such things would be a lie at this point, no matter how deeply felt it was by the individuals employing it.

Read the Word

Therefore each of you must put off falsehood and speak truthfully to your neighbor, for we are all members of one body.
Ephesians 4:25

Think It Over

We are all members of one body. What is that about? These words were written for husbands and wives, children and parents, brothers and sisters in Christ in the ancient Greek city of Ephesus. As members of one church, they were members of one "body"—namely, the body of Christ. The body of the church has truths to tell as well, just as our physical bodies do.

Since we have recommended that pure and healthy friendship dating should take place with other followers of Christ, the final words of the verse from Ephesians add a nice touch to this day's theme: "Tell the truth to each other with your bodies, for we are all members of one body." We are mysteriously connected with one another in more ways than we

know. Therefore we must treat one another with honesty and honor, since in doing so we are also showing our love to Christ himself.

Talk It Over

- Make up a question for your conversation partner based on the issue of telling the truth with one's body.

- Now answer your conversation partner's question for you.

Pray It Forward

Jesus, since you are the Truth, live powerfully in me to help me live truthfully with others. I hold up before you my relationships of all kinds. Help me to understand what they are all about and to live in harmony with that truth. Amen.

DAY 5:
A REPORT CARD ON LOVE
Week 3: HOW DO YOU GROW IN TRUE FRIENDSHIP?

Imagine that people received report cards from heaven every now and then—maybe about as often as school report cards. The one subject this semester? True Friendship 101. The marks breakdown: 5 percent for homework, 5 percent for projects, and 90 percent for participation and attitude. There are no exams. The course criteria: 1 Corinthians 13. The course instructor: the Holy Spirit.

If you are in a dating relationship right now, or even just a regular friendship with another girl or guy, complete a self-assessment for the last semester of true friendship. Give yourself a mark of A, B, C, or D for each category of 1 Corinthians 13. Use pluses and minuses if necessary to make it more precise.

Read the Word 📖

Criterion	Mark
Love is patient,	_____
love is kind.	_____
It does not envy,	_____
it does not boast,	_____
it is not proud.	_____
It does not dishonor others,	_____
it is not self-seeking,	_____
it is not easily angered,	_____
it keeps no record of wrongs.	_____
Love does not delight in evil	_____
but rejoices with the truth.	_____
It always protects,	_____
always trusts,	_____
always hopes,	_____
always perseveres.	_____

1 Corinthians 13:4–7

If getting good marks is your thing, figure out your grade point average for love based on this semester's work.

Talk It Over

- How do your results compare with your conversation partner's? (Everyone likes to see what the other person got, right?)

- Where would you say you need to put in some extra work in this course (maybe with some after-hours tutoring)?

Listen Up 🎧
Find a popular song that uses any words or phrases from 1 Corinthians 13 in its lyrics, and share it with your conversation partner.

Think It Over
The good news at the end of this course on true love is that "love never fails" (1 Corinthians 13:8). Now that could have a couple different meanings in this context!

Pray It Forward 🙏
Write your final prayer for these first three weeks of partner conversations. What do you want to remember about the first curriculum theme, "Practicing Friendship"? What are you thankful for? How do you want to grow further? Whom in your life do you want to bless and encourage? Jesus asked a certain beggar named Bartimaeus, "What do you want me to do for you?" (Mark 10:51). Suppose he is asking you the same question today. What do you say?

CHOOSING LIFE

CONVERSATION 1

WHY AM I HERE?
HOW OUR WORLDVIEW
SHAPES OUR CHOICES

GROUP SESSION

What "floats your boat"? Where do you find meaning, joy, value, and purpose in life? How you answer these questions gives a clue as to what kinds of pressure you would feel if you ever became a teenager who was expecting a baby but didn't want to be.

We're not introducing this conversation because we think you're going to end up facing that dilemma. We just know that it's valuable for everyone to think carefully through such matters, both for their own hearts and the hearts of those they influence.

In today's session we look at values, influences, and pressures related to the issue of unwanted pregnancy and the issue of abortion.

REEL to REAL

1. **Bobbi tells Jesse that she is pregnant**

- What did you notice in this scene? How do you feel about the conversation?

- Jesse tells Bobbi, "Having a baby would probably screw up your life right now." What does he mean by that?

- Bobbi throws the same challenge back at Jesse: "Wouldn't a baby mess up your life too?" What are some of the ways that might be true?

- Jesse says, "You're the one who's pregnant." What does he mean by that? Is he right?

- What underlying values are implied in this conversation, and how do they pressure Bobbi?

2. Bobbi tells her parents

- What would it be like to tell news like this to your parents? What approach would you take, and what response would you hope to get?

- What is Pastor Ryan most upset about? What might people in his church say or do as a result of Bobbi's pregnancy?

- What kind of pressure does his response put on Bobbi?

- What do you think is more important for Christians (including pastors) to be "experts" at: living without making mistakes or showing mercy to those who make mistakes?

3. Grace speaks of the Creator

- What is one word, phrase, or image Grace uses that sticks in your mind?

- If we view the universe as a random, purposeless occurrence, which lives are worth protecting?

- If we view the world as created by a loving God who pays attention to the smallest detail, how does that affect our attitude toward pregnancy and abortion?

 ENGAGE THE WORD

With your small group, prepare a brief creative presentation of the text assigned you. For example, you could read your scripture together while dramatizing it wi hand actions, or one person could read while the others act out a moving or froz picture of the meaning.

- Genesis 2:15
- Acts 17:26–27
- 1 Corinthians 10:31
- John 15:4
- Colossians 3:17

- Philippians 4:4
- 1 Thessalonians 5:16–18
- John 13:34
- Matthew 22:37–39
- Ephesians 5:1–2

DAY 1:
A GOD OF DETAILS
Week 4: WHY AM I HERE?

When was the last time you looked at a baby picture of yourself? Were you born with a striking headful of hair, or were you born bald? Either way, you were born with all the hair follicles you were ever going to have. (Those are the tiny sheaths in your skin that produce hair of various thicknesses, colors, and lengths). And even if you were bald at birth, you had lots of hair all over your body before you were born. It just fell off while you were still inside your mother's womb.

There are about 100,000 hairs on the average human head, and about 5,000,000 more covering the rest of our bodies (except on the palms of our hands and the soles of our feet), including many hairs we can't even see. Jesus had something to say about hair.

Read the Word

There was a time when thousands of people had gathered around Jesus—so many that they were trampling each other. He said something encouraging to his followers that day regarding the smallest details of life in this world.

With your conversation partner, take turns reading aloud the following words of the Lord.

Are not five sparrows sold for two pennies? Yet not one of them is forgotten by God. Indeed, the very

hairs of your head are all numbered. Don't be afraid; you are worth more than many sparrows.
Luke 12:6-7

Nothing escapes the attention of our loving God, who pays attention to the smallest details of life. In God's worldview, even sparrows matter. And you matter even more.

Talk It Over 💬

- What other unexpected body parts and creatures do you think God keeps track of?

- How does God remember so much?

- Why would God care about these seemingly minor details of his universe?

- Does every single thing in the universe have the same worth to God?

MEME-orize It 🖼
Take a photo or find an image of a child or adult with a really interesting hairstyle and caption it with Jesus's words, "The very hairs of your head are all numbered" (Luke 12:7). Share your meme with your conversation partner and somebody else.

Listen Up 🎧
On YouTube, see if you can find a recording of someone singing the song, "His Eye Is On the Sparrow."

Pray It Forward 🙏
Write and speak a short prayer of thanksgiving to God for his loving care over three small, unusual, but not insignificant areas of your life.

Dear God, thank you for knowing, remembering, and caring all about:

DAY 2:
THE GOD OF THE VULNERABLE
Week 4: WHY AM I HERE?

The last time we see Grácia, Chase, and OB sitting by the island campfire in the movie, Grácia says with confidence, "God loves Bobbi. He loves me." Her idea about the kind of God who rules the universe comes from her own experience of being loved and cared for when she was most vulnerable.

It's no accident she experienced this kind of love. Since ancient times, God's people have sung about his special focus on the weak and needy.

Read the Word

Take turns with your conversation partner reading aloud these declarations from Scripture:

The Lord is close to the brokenhearted and saves those who are crushed in spirit.
Psalm 34:18

The Lord watches over the foreigner and sustains the fatherless and the widow, but he frustrates the ways of the wicked.
Psalm 146:9

A father to the fatherless, a defender of widows, is God in his holy dwelling. God sets the lonely in families, he leads out the prisoners with singing; but the rebellious live in a sun-scorched land.
Psalm 68:5–6

For this is what the high and exalted One says—he who lives forever, whose name is holy: "I live in a high and holy place, but also with the one who is contrite and lowly in spirit, to revive the spirit of the lowly and to revive the heart of the contrite."
Isaiah 57:15

Play It Over ▶

Play a quick sketching game with your conversation partner. Take 30 seconds to sketch a phrase (picture only, no words) from anywhere in one of these verses. If your partner guesses it, you get a point. Play until someone reaches 3 points. (Obviously, this one only works if you're with your partner or video-chatting.)

Talk It Over 💬

- How does a person become crushed in spirit? Give a real-life example.

- Who are the "fatherless" in our society?

- God seems to be most interested in the people the world is least interested in. Who would you say are the "lowliest" people in our present world?

- Why does God live in such different (i.e., high and low) places as these?

Pray It Forward

Complete these sentences and read them aloud as a prayer:

God, I feel most proud and rebellious when . . .

I feel most lowly when . . .

I bring to you all of who I am and ask you to change me, live with me, and live in me. Amen.

DAY 3:
SEEING THE WORLD UPSIDE-DOWN
Week 4: WHY AM I HERE?

Some people say that standing on your head for a couple minutes a day is good for you. They say it builds core muscle strength, improves blood flow to the brain and endocrine glands, and reduces stress, among other things. Too bad it's not easier to do!

There may be something to the idea of getting an "inverted" perspective on life on a regular basis. In a way, reading the Bible every day is like a spiritual version of standing on your head. Not only does it take practice and improve health, but also it brings everything around you into an immediate new perspective. Like these next words of the apostle Paul do.

Read the Word 📖
Read in unison with your conversation partner.

God chose the foolish things of the world to shame the wise; God chose the weak things of the world to shame the strong. God chose the lowly things of this world and the despised things—and the things that are not—to nullify the things that are, so that no one may boast before him.
1 Corinthians 1:27–29

Think It Over

These words to the Christians at Corinth stand the world itself on its head. They speak of a different value system than we are used to in everyday life.

How might God's value system help us look at a situation like Bobbi's in a new way? A girl in high school becomes pregnant by accident. If she goes ahead and has the baby, it might "screw up her life," as her boyfriend puts it. It might trap her for a long time. Maybe it's wisest to just quietly make the problem disappear.

The growth of a new human being after conception is so tiny and hidden that it's easy to think of the unborn as one of those "things that are not." But God actually chooses the "things that are not," our scripture passage says. He assigns them a value above "the things that are"— above all that the world values most. In Bobbi's case, that would include her education, finances, family life, social life, career path, even her personal reputation. As important as these things seem, they do not exceed the value of a tiny human life.

Talk It Over 💬

- What inspires you in these words of Scripture?

- What, if anything, unsettles you about them?

- Is God resentful of the wise and strong? Why doesn't he want people to "boast before him"? How does all this relate to his love for us?

Play It Over ▶

Test your partner's memory of today's scripture passage. Read it out loud for them, pausing wherever there is an interesting adjective (a descriptive word). For example, say, "God chose the _____ things of the world to shame the _____." See if your partner can fill in the blanks as you go. Act out a clue for the missing word if they get stuck.

Pray It Forward 🙏

Praise God for his perfect wisdom and powerful love. Ask him to shape your worldview into the same pattern as his so that you can live in the love, truth, and joy that stands the world on its head.

DAY 4:
WELCOMING THE GREATEST
Week 4: WHY AM I HERE?

When you're part of a team or a class or any other group, you sometimes start to wonder what your place is in relation to others. There may be an obvious "pecking order," which starts from the best player, smartest student, toughest gang member, etc., and goes on down. Or the ranking system may be less obvious.

In the movie we see OB wondering about his rank in the school environment in terms of grades and friendships. And we see Josie, the leader of the "cool girls," trying to maintain a certain status that is threatened when Grácia arrives.

It was no different for the team Jesus built, the one we call the twelve disciples. On several occasions they started to get a little edgy about their status in relation to each other. Check out this example.

Read the Word 📖

The partner with the highest rank can read aloud the text for today. (Just kidding. Toss a coin.)

At that time the disciples came to Jesus and asked, "Who, then, is the greatest in the kingdom of heaven?"

He called a little child to him, and placed the child among them. And
he said: "Truly I tell you, unless you change and become like little children, you will never enter the kingdom of heaven. Therefore, whoever takes the lowly position of this child is the greatest in the kingdom of heaven. And whoever welcomes one such child in my name welcomes me."
Matthew 18:1–5

Talk It Over

- What do you think it means to change and become like little children?

- Jesus says that when we welcome a little child in his name, we welcome him. Why would that be?

- Do you think that we also welcome Jesus when we welcome an unborn child in his name?

MEME-orize It

Find a picture of a small child and put it side by side with a picture of someone the world considers great (for example, an athlete, celebrity, or world leader). Caption your image with the words, "Who is the greatest in the kingdom of heaven?" Share it with your conversation partner and somebody else.

Ask A Mentor

Choose a trusted older person and ask them "What do you think Jesus meant when he said we wouldn't enter the kingdom of heaven unless we become like little children?"

Try It Out ✔

Sometime in the next day or week when you meet a small child, look at him or her and say in the quietness of your heart, "Welcome, in the name of Jesus." If you know the child personally, get down on their level, take their hands, look into their eyes, and say the words out loud. See what happens.

Pray It Forward

Jesus, the area of my life where I most worry about my "greatness," or lack thereof, in the world's eyes is this:

Thank you, Lord, that this kind of greatness is not what you require from me to live as a beloved citizen of your kingdom. Make me humble enough to accept your loving welcome and to welcome others too. Amen.

DAY 5:
ENDING SHAME
Week 4: WHY AM I HERE?

Christian communities should be the safest places in the world to admit mistakes. Christians know well that each of us has sinned and no one has the right to cast the first stone. But even more, Christians ought to be "safe people" because of our deep trust in the redemptive creativity of God that can bring good from every calamity.

Unfortunately, we don't always get it right—as we see with Bobbi's dad when she tells him she's pregnant. In that moment of shock in the family living room, he gets more caught up in the possible threat to his reputation as a pastor than in the painful dilemma his daughter is experiencing. He doesn't realize how his stressed, anxious response may pressure Bobbi to take desperate measures.

As a minister of Jesus and the Word, Pastor Ryan needs to remember at this moment how God's redeeming grace is ready to flood in at our darkest moments. We see that pattern again and again in Scripture, especially in the writings of the Old Testament prophets. One minute they're talking about all the terrible things going on and the next minute they're saying, "Nevertheless, God is going to come through and turn things around for you before you know it."

Read the Word 📖

Here are some words of God that a young person like Bobbi might find encouraging amid the kind of crisis she's experiencing. Read them out loud twice with your conversation partner:

Do not be afraid; you will not be put to shame. Do not fear disgrace, you will not be humiliated. You will forget the shame of your youth.
Isaiah 54:4

These words were written to the people of Israel about their troubled relationship with God, but they also reveal something in general about the attitude of God's heart toward his beloved ones. He doesn't want to hold us in shame like a bully holding someone's head underwater. He wants to remove shame from us altogether. That's one of the things Jesus did on the cross: He took all the shame and sin of the world onto himself on our behalf.

Now God wants his people to wipe away shame as well. Read some more words of Scripture together:

Be kind and compassionate to one another, forgiving each other, just as in Christ God forgave you.
Ephesians 4:32

Talk It Over 💬

- What kinds of things do you remember being ashamed of when you were a child?

- Do you think people experience shame more often, or less often, once they become teenagers?

- At what time of your life—past, present, or future—would you most want to hear the words from Isaiah 54:4 spoken to your heart by the Holy Spirit?

- If Bobbi's father had been kind and compassionate after hearing her news, what difference might that have made to her next course of action?

Ask A Mentor

Find a trusted older person to answer this question: "When you were young, did you ever have to admit something really difficult to your parents? What did they say? How did things turn out?"

Try It Out ✔

If someone slights you this week, try forgiving them on the spot without trying to make them feel bad about it.

Pray It Forward 🙏

Tell Jesus about an area of your life in the past or present where you have experienced shame.

Now imagine him walking up, taking that shame off you, putting it on himself, and walking a long path to the cross.

Thank him for what he has done for us. Pray for someone else who might be struggling with shame right now.

CONVERSATION 2

WHAT SHOULD I DO?

FACING THE CRISIS OF
UNEXPECTED PREGNANCY

GROUP SESSION

We exist because other people conceived us and chose to give us life. In this session we want to encourage everyone to cherish the lives of human beings from the very beginning of their existence, the same way God does.

REEL to REAL

- How many people here like going to the doctor? Why?

- How many people *don't* like going to the doctor? Why not?

1. Bobbi sees a doctor

- What's going on in Bobbi's mind and heart during this conversation with the doctor?

- Is Bobbi expecting to be pregnant or not expecting to be pregnant?

- Has anyone here ever heard upsetting news from a doctor (or someone else)? What is that like?

1. Bobbi gets her test result

- Describe Bobbi's reaction to the test result in a single word. Do you think the fact that she is a Christian plays into her reaction?

- As the doctor outlines 3 different options for her, what do you imagine is going through Bobbi's mind?

- Does the doctor try to sway her in any direction?

- As Bobbi moves on from this appointment, what specific questions will she be asking herself?

- Last week we talked about some of the reasons people might not want to have a baby as a teenager. What are some of the positive reasons a person would want to have a baby, even under circumstances like these?

ENGAGE THE WORD

Your small group will be assigned one of these scriptures for an activity that considers facts about prenatal development. Once you have been assigned a text, choose an interesting fact from the handout your leader gave you that relates to your scripture. Prepare to read your scripture in unison as a group, and choose one person who will read the development fact.

Your group's scripture will be one of the following:

- Psalm 139:13
- Psalm 139:14
- Psalm 139:15
- Psalm 139:16
- Isaiah 49:1
- Jeremiah 1:5
- Psalm 22:9
- Psalm 22:10
- Luke 1:41–42
- Luke 1:44
- Genesis 1:26
- Genesis 1:27
- Luke 18:16
- Matthew 18:5

DAY 1:
CHILDREN CHANGE HISTORY
Week 5: WHAT SHOULD I DO?

"Wouldn't a baby mess up *your* life right now too?" Bobbi says to Jesse while they are talking on the phone about her unexpected pregnancy.

"Yeah, I guess so," he says. "I haven't thought about it much. You just told me five minutes ago!"

Children don't just change individual lives. They change history. The unexpected conception of a child by a pair of teenagers isn't an issue only for the young woman carrying the baby. Bobbi is quite right to put the ball back into Jesse's court the way she does. This child will be his child too, after all. He will have to acknowledge a certain moral and relational responsibility, even a financial one, for both baby and mother. As a young man in high school, is he ready for that?

The impulse is strong for Jesse to urge Bobbi toward abortion. Even if he hasn't had a chance to think things over yet, he senses what a tremendous disruption a new baby would bring to his life.

Do you know that when Jesus was a baby, he was thought of in the same way as Bobbi and Jesse's child? In Jesus's case, it was with even greater fear and concern—since the response to pregnancy outside of marriage was harsh during Mary and Joseph's time.

Mysterious visitors to Jerusalem heralded the birth of the new king of the Jews, and suddenly Jesus became a baby who was going to "mess up" the life of a very important person: King Herod, the current king of the Jews. He tried to find out where Jesus was, but got zero cooperation from the foreign visitors. So Herod did a desperate thing. He decided he would try to change history himself.

Read the Word

When Herod realized that he had been outwitted by the Magi, he was furious, and he gave orders to kill all the boys in Bethlehem and its vicinity who were two years old and under, in accordance with the time he had learned from the Magi. Then what was said through the prophet Jeremiah was fulfilled: "A voice is heard in Ramah, weeping and great mourning, Rachel weeping for her children and refusing to be comforted, because they are no more."
Matthew 2:16–18

Jesus escaped the massacre because an angel told his father to wake up their family in the middle of the night and leave the country. Needless to say, we are grateful Jesus was not killed by Herod's soldiers, but we grieve that so many other little ones were lost. It must have been a horrific event with far-reaching consequences. The many infants murdered in Bethlehem never got a chance to make their own mark on history, apart from the deep sadness their parents and families must have felt over their loss.

Talk It Over

Some might say, "There's no comparison between the slaughter of the innocents in Bethlehem and the practice of abortion in our day and age." What do you think? What are the differences and what are the similarities?

Look It Up 🔍

Other than abortion, what other serious threats exist to the lives of babies and little children in our world today?

Pray It Forward 🙏

Ask Jesus, brother of the slain infants of Bethlehem, to preserve tiny lives in our world that they might leave their good mark on history. Invite him to use your life for the same purpose, if he so chooses.

DAY 2:
CRY OUT
Week 5: WHAT SHOULD I DO?

When Bobbi's painful phone call with Jesse comes to an end, we are left with an image of her weeping on the bed, as though from the viewpoint of angels above her. Although she loves him, she has realized he isn't willing to take responsibility for what has happened. ("You're the one who's pregnant!" he has just said.) She must feel incredibly alone at this moment.

What might be going through her mind? What might she be seeing in her imagination? Is there any place she can pour her heartbreak where it can be received, comforted, and even healed?

The psalms say that there is. The poems of love, fear, joy, and anxiety in the middle of the Bible cover pretty much every emotion known to humankind—from raging anger to gentle bliss, with various stops in between. The underlying message of this 150-chapter-strong collection of ancient spoken-word poetry is that whatever a person is experiencing should be lifted up to God in worship and as worship. Even the heaviest experiences of life deserve to be spoken out. As difficult as it may be to lift them up to God, the words of the psalms are there to help us when we can't find our own words to use.

Read the Word

With your conversation partner, take turns testing out some words of the psalms. You might want to try holding up your hands in front of you while you read, as though lifting up the words in them.

I am worn out from my groaning. All night long I flood my bed with weeping and drench my couch with tears.
Psalm 6:6

How long, Lord? Will you forget me forever? How long will you hide your face from me? How long must I wrestle with my thoughts and day after day have sorrow in my heart?
Psalm 13:1–2

Do not be far from me, for trouble is near and there is no one to help.
Psalm 22:11

Turn to me and be gracious to me, for I am lonely and afflicted. Relieve the troubles of my heart and free me from my anguish. Look on my affliction and my distress and take away all my sins.
Psalm 25:16–18

Hear my cry for mercy as I call to you for help, as I lift up my hands toward your Most Holy Place.
Psalm 28:2

Jesus himself expressed emotional agony of this kind when he was in the garden of Gethsemane just before his arrest and crucifixion. He told his friends, "My soul is overwhelmed with sorrow to the point of death" (Matthew 26:38). His struggle was different from that of a young person facing the consequences of a life-changing mistake, but his struggle still provides a model for anyone suffering with the dread of something they cannot avoid.

Jesus fell facedown and prayed, "My Father, if it is possible, may this cup be taken from me. Yet not as I will, but as you will." Again he prayed, "My Father, if it is possible, may this cup be taken from me. Yet not as I will, but as you will" (Matthew 26:39). Without taking away from the profound sorrow of our Lord on his way to the cross, we could agree that a pregnant girl might be similarly afraid about going through with a pregnancy she was not expecting. And that's exactly the kind of sorrow God wants to hear about.

"Cast all your anxiety on him," Scripture says, "because he cares for you" (1 Peter 5:7).

Talk It Over 💬

- When in your life have you felt the most alone?

- When in your life were you the most afraid of something difficult you had to do?

- Have you ever prayed a prayer like this: "May this cup be taken from me"? What happened?

Ask A Mentor ❓
Try out today's "Talk It Over" questions on a trusted adult.

Try It Out ✔
The next time you feel abandoned or afraid, try opening your Bible to the book of Psalms and finding some words that express the mood of your heart. Read them over to yourself a few times until you remember them, and then carry them with you as go through the rest of your day.

Pray It Forward 🙏
What are you facing in your life right now that you might want to pour out to God? Write a prayer about it here.

DAY 3:
GOD WILL SHOW THE WAY
Week 5: WHAT SHOULD I DO?

"When I was little, I thought abortion was evil," Bobbi tells Grace. "But now . . ."

Just speaking these things out loud to another person is such a healthy step for her.

"I honestly don't know what to do."

Grácia doesn't tell her what to do at that moment, even though she might want to. Instead, she directs Bobbi to God, which is exactly the right approach. God, the Maker, Knower, and Lover of the child in the womb, can best convince Bobbi of the right way to go.

We've just discussed how the psalms give us permission to express whatever we feel—but they don't stop there. They also assure us that God receives those feelings and gives us back real-life answers. That's important, since our feelings are often linked to particular questions, needs, and requests.

Read the Word 📖
You know the routine. Take turns with your conversation partner reading these expressions of longing for and trust in God's guidance.

Show me your ways, Lord, teach me your paths. Guide me in your truth and teach me, for you are God my Savior, and my hope is in you all day long.
Psalm 25:4–5

I remain confident of this: I will see the goodness of the Lord in the land of the living. Wait for the Lord; be strong and take heart and wait for the Lord.
Psalm 27:13–14

The Lord will work out his plans for my life—for your faithful love, O Lord, endures forever.
Psalm 138:8 NLT

God wants to show us the way. He answers our trust—even our doubt and confusion—with assurances that he will lead us through the big decisions and practical details of our lives.

The next scriptures present the voice of God answering his people. Read them aloud to each other, leaving a little space in between to let them sink in.

I will instruct you and teach you in the way you should go; I will counsel you with my loving eye on you.
Psalm 32:8-9

Whether you turn to the right or to the left, your ears will hear a voice behind you, saying, "This is the way; walk in it."
Isaiah 30:21

When you pass through the waters I will be with you; and when you pass through the rivers, they will not sweep over you. When you walk through the fire, you will not be burned; the flames will not set you ablaze. For I am the Lord your God, the Holy One of Israel, your Savior.
Isaiah 43:2-3

Talk It Over

- Which of the scriptures for today most connects with you, and why?

- Have you ever received a clear sense from God of what you should do at a time when you really needed help? Describe the situation and what came of it.

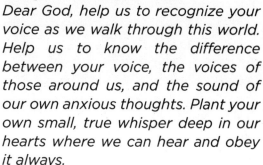

Try It Out ✔

Choose a verse from the first set of texts, write it on a sticky note, and put it on a mirror in your home. Choose a verse from the second set of texts, do the same thing, and put it on the inside of a door that leads out of your home.

Pray It Forward

Dear God, help us to recognize your voice as we walk through this world. Help us to know the difference between your voice, the voices of those around us, and the sound of our own anxious thoughts. Plant your own small, true whisper deep in our hearts where we can hear and obey it always.

DAY 4:
THE PLAN IS GOOD
Week 5: WHAT SHOULD I DO?

Sometimes it takes a long time for life to make sense. "Why did that have to happen?" we say. "Why did you let that happen?" we say to God. "Why did I ever do such a thing?" we say to ourselves.

Years down the road, we may get the beginning of an answer to questions like these. We never actually find out what life would have been like if we had made another choice, but we do find out some of the good things God has brought about through what took place.

Consider the story of Cindy Anderson, for example, as presented in the video testimony for the last group session. A pastor's daughter in the same dilemma as Bobbi Ryan, Cindy kept her baby as a teenager and now admires her son's wide-reaching ministry as a youth pastor. His presence in her family home as a young child helped heal her troubled relationship with her dad. We see that God worked good even after Cindy's hopes for her life went sideways.

A dramatic biblical example of this kind of thing is the Old Testament story of Joseph. There must have been times when Joseph's life felt to him like a disaster in comparison to how he had originally imagined it would turn out. He had not counted on being sold as a slave to a desert caravan by his resentful older brothers or being framed for attempted rape and thrown into prison in Egypt. Then again, he had not counted on being put in charge of a whole nation either—which is what it all led to in the end.

Years later, Joseph bumped into his brothers again, the ones responsible for his painful detour. It gave him a chance to reflect on how God had used the difficult circumstances of his life for a higher design.

Read the Word 📖

Joseph said to his brothers, "I am Joseph! Is my father still living?" But his brothers were not able to answer him, because they were terrified at his presence.

Then Joseph said to his brothers, "Come close to me." When they had done so, he said, "I am your brother Joseph, the one you sold into Egypt! And now, do not be distressed and do not be angry with yourselves for selling me here, because it was to save lives that God sent me ahead of you. For two years now there has been famine in the land, and for the next five years there will be no plowing and reaping. But God sent me ahead of you to preserve for you a remnant on earth and to save your lives by a great deliverance.

"So then, it was not you who sent me here, but God."
Genesis 45:3–8

Talk It Over 💬

- After Joseph revealed himself to his brothers, Genesis 45:14–15 tells us that he embraced his brothers and cried at their presence. Why didn't Joseph take revenge on them?

- Romans 8:28 says, "And we know that in all things God works for the good of those who love him, who have been called according to his purpose." Think up a painful, disturbing, or surprising life situation people experience to which this verse can apply.

- If God brings ultimate good out of the problems, errors, and mishaps of our life, does that mean he made those troubles happen in the first place? What do you think?

Think It Over

At the end of a heart-to-heart conversation with Bobbi, Grácia tells her, "We have to believe he has a plan." It's not that she's urging Bobbi to engage in wishful thinking. She is sharing the reassuring truth of the One who is never taken by surprise. Like a skilled composer, God can work any snippet of melody, no matter how dissonant or offbeat, back into the larger, beautiful symphony of the world's redemption. How does he do that?

Pray It Forward

Thank God for something difficult in your life these days.

God, you are so creative. I thank you that this is happening to me right now, since it gives you one more interesting way to work for my good and, through me, the good of others.

DAY 5:
CHOOSE LIFE
Week 5: WHAT SHOULD I DO?

Would you believe it? God is pro-choice. That may sound shocking, but it's true. God doesn't favor abortion, and he isn't pleased with every single choice human beings make, but God is in favor of the *opportunity* to make a choice. Opportunity to choose is foundational to the world he created, which he didn't fill with drones, clones, or puppets but with free beings made in his own image.

Such freedom to choose involves great risk, since human beings can choose to do destructive things to themselves and others. But such freedom is also the soil in which true love grows, making it worth the risk. In other words, it's worth having a world in which people may choose *not* to love, in order to have a world in which they may choose to love wholeheartedly.

One of the loose ends in the movie is the character of Jesse. At the end of the film we see a brief image of Bobbi interacting with her lovely daughter—a sign of God's redemption. But what about Jesse? Will he ever choose to contribute to his child's life? Should he get a fresh opportunity to take responsibility? It would be just like God to give him one.

Read the Word

Jesse would benefit from a genuine encounter with the God of true choice and true life. Then he might be able to take words like these to heart.

Read these verses through twice with your conversation partner.

This is what the Lord says: "Stand at the crossroads and look; ask for the ancient paths, ask where the good way is, and walk in it, and you will find rest for your souls."
Jeremiah 6:16

The alternative to a rested soul is an anguished soul. Whenever we choose against life as God purposes it, there is a painful result. That's what Moses tells the children of Israel when they are at a crossroads on the edge of the Promised Land. He describes in detail the terrible consequences that will follow if they break the terms of their covenant of obedience with God.

Read the conclusion of Moses's sermon with your conversation partner.

This day I call the heavens and the earth as witnesses against you that I have set before you life and death, blessings and curses. Now choose life, so that you and your children may live and that you may love the Lord your God, listen to his voice, and

hold fast to him. For the Lord is your life, and he will give you many years in the land he swore to give to your fathers, Abraham, Isaac and Jacob.
Deuteronomy 30:19–20

Think It Over

"Choose life." The words could easily be applied to the crisis of unplanned pregnancy. God may be pro-choice, but even more importantly, God is pro-life. That's why God's Son said what he did: "I have come that they may have life, and have it to the full" (John 10:10).

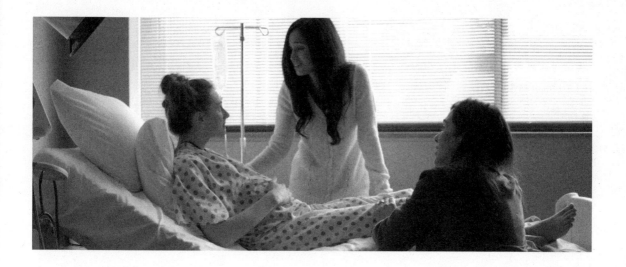

Talk It Over 💬

- Are you at any kind of crossroads right now?

- What would it mean to "choose life"?

- What would "rest for your soul" look and feel like?

Pray It Forward 🙏

Dear God, I choose you and your good way. Thank you for welcoming me into a free, loving relationship with you. I receive with open hands the full life that you choose for me. In Jesus's name, amen.

CONVERSATION 3

HOW CAN I HELP?

SUPPORTING OTHERS IN
CHOOSING LIFE

GROUP SESSION

Even if we never find ourselves in Bobbi Ryan's shoes, many of us will encounter friends who face life-and-death decisions and a difficult road ahead no matter what choice they make. What kind of love and support will we provide? What grace and healing will we speak? As Grace models so beautifully in the movie, and as a well-known Bible story character does as well, we can learn to reach out and encourage others that a loving, forgiving God has a good plan for everyone in every situation.

 **REEL to REAL**

1. Grace meets with Bobbi

- Why does Bobbi feel safe talking about her dilemma with Grace?

- How does Grace demonstrate friendship, care, and love in this conversation? What does she do? What does she not do?

- What does Grace say about God, and how might this help Bobbi?

2. Looking for Bobbi

- Why are Bobbi's parents looking for her so anxiously? In what ways can having an abortion harm a young woman?

- Why do you think Bobbi decides to go to the abortion clinic after all? How is she feeling on the way there?

- Grace, Chase, and OB take the risk of leaving school in the middle of class to go and find Bobbi. Do you think this is the right thing to do? What will they say or do when they find her?

2. Outside the abortion clinic

- When Bobbi comes out of the clinic, what do you think has happened? What is Pastor Ryan thinking?

- What does Pastor Ryan realize about his relationship with his daughter as he stands facing her? In what way does he choose life?

- Does the reconciliation between Pastor Ryan and Bobbi depend on whether or not she has had an abortion?

- Why do you think Bobbi couldn't go through with it?

- What if this story turned out differently and Bobbi came out of the clinic no longer pregnant. What would you want to see happen in that case, and why?

- At the end of the movie, Grace accompanies Bobbi in the birthing room. Would you have the courage to do that for a friend?

ENGAGE THE WORD
Today's key scripture covers the story of the good Samaritan (Luke 10:25-37)—one of Jesus's most famous parables. As you read and discuss this story, consider how you could imagine this story playing out in modern-day situations.

 CARRY IT OUT

As a conclusion to the "Choosing Life" theme, take action in some way described by this list:

- Explore the websites of organizations that advocate for the unborn (such as Students for Life), assist pregnant young people (such as National Institute of Family and Life Advocates), or minister healing to those who had abortions that they now regret (such as Silent No More).

- Research the history of abortion in America.

- Find out more about abortion in your region: What laws govern it? How much does it cost, and who pays for it?

- Hold a drive for baby items (e.g., diapers, bedding, sleepers) for a local crisis pregnancy center or youth maternity home.

- Befriend a teen mom or dad.

- Babysit for a single mom.

- Befriend an elderly person who lacks quality relationships.

- Try to locate a program that serves vulnerable or disadvantaged children and consider volunteering there.

DAY 1:
COMFORT MY PEOPLE
Week 6: HOW CAN I HELP?

A couple of weeks ago, we discussed Pastor Ryan's stressed-out response to Bobbi's announcement of her pregnancy. Even as her mother reaches out instinctively to put her arm around her, Bobbi says to her father in anger, "I'm pregnant, and you're the one who needs consoling? I hate you. I *hate* you!" What a shattering moment in her family's life.

Young people and parents undergoing a crisis like this need comfort. They need to be held tightly. They need to hear words of hope that can bind up their broken hearts. They need to receive practical support from God's people, through whom he puts his loving-kindness into action. The Bible gives many descriptions of this role.

Read the Word 📖

Take turns reading these texts with your conversation partner.

Praise be to the God and Father of our Lord Jesus Christ, the Father of compassion and the God of all comfort, who comforts us in all our troubles, so that we can comfort those in any trouble with the comfort we ourselves receive from God.
2 Corinthians 1:3–4

The Spirit of the Sovereign Lord is on me, because the Lord has anointed meto proclaim good news to the poor. He has sent me to bind up the brokenhearted.
Isaiah 61:1

Each one will be like a shelter from the wind and a refuge from the storm, like streams of water in the desert and the shadow of a great rock in a thirsty land.
Isaiah 32:2

Comfort, comfort my people, says your God.
Isaiah 40:1

Talk It Over 💬

- How is the first text, about comforting others with the comfort we have received, especially true of Grácia in the movie?

- What kind of good news might a pregnant teen, her family, and her boyfriend need to hear?

- In a practical sense, what might a "shelter from the wind" or a "refuge from the storm" look like for a desperate young person?

Try It Out ✔

Go outside your usual comfort zone. Talk to somebody this week who might need a comforting word.

Pray It Forward 🙏

Pray together for someone you know who needs the comfort of the Holy Spirit and the comfort of God's people.

DAY 2:
CARRY THE MAT TOGETHER
Week 6: HOW CAN I HELP?

Even though Scripture gives us pictures of the lone servant of the Lord, anointed by the Spirit to bind up the brokenhearted, the followers of Jesus often care for others as a team.

Loving others in practical ways can be hard work. Not only do we need to pool resources, skills, and ideas as we do so, but also we need to share loving mutual support with those who are helping.

Grace takes advantage of this strength of togetherness with Chase and OB when Bobbi's situation is weighing on her one night. "My heart's just hurting for somebody right now. Do you mind if I play something?" She sings a song of comfort and encouragement for Bobbi from afar. Even though she can't give details of the situation to the guys at this time, she is sharing the burden with them as much as she can.

A few days later, when Bobbi is at the abortion clinic on the brink of a life-altering decision, Grace leans on the friends again to accompany her. That's the way it should be. Though we may sometimes be tempted to act as lone heroes on behalf of others, we need each other.

There's a lovely story of this kind of joint action in Mark's Gospel.

Read the Word 📖

A few days later, when Jesus again entered Capernaum, the people heard that he had come home. They gathered in such large numbers that there was no room left, not even outside the door, and he preached the word to them. Some men came, bringing to him a paralyzed man, carried by four of them. Since they could not get him to Jesus because of the crowd, they made an opening in the roof above Jesus by digging through it and then lowered the mat the man was lying on. When Jesus saw their faith, he said to the paralyzed man, "Son, your sins are forgiven."
Mark 2:1–5

Think It Over

Many paralytics can't go places on their own. They rely entirely on others. This can be true of people in a spiritual sense as well. They might have the idea of going to Jesus for help, but there's no way they can get there on their own steam. That's where the bold initiative of friends comes in.

The friends of the paralytic in this story have set their minds on helping. Not put off by the impossibility of bringing him to Jesus through the front door, they decide to come through the roof instead. Who cares if they make fools of themselves? The important thing is to get their friend into the presence of the One who can truly help him. They don't give Jesus instructions as to what they want; they just put their friend in front of him and look at Jesus

with hope. It's a beautiful model of cooperative prayer.

The text says that Jesus "saw their faith." We can only guess what the paralyzed man was feeling, hoping, and wondering amid this hubbub. Whatever it was, we see that the faith of friends was important to Jesus—a kind of trigger for his action. "Son, your sins are forgiven." Wow—no one even asked for that! They brought him for physical healing and he ended up receiving spiritual healing first.

We didn't read to the end of the story, but rest assured that Jesus heals the man's physical paralysis as well—in spite of the disapproval of local religious leaders. To the amazement of everybody, the man goes out walking, carrying his own mat.

Talk It Over 💬

- Have you ever felt paralyzed, unable to get to Jesus on your own? Or have you known a friend in such a condition?

- How does a person become paralyzed in a spiritual sense?

- How might a young person who has chosen to have an abortion fit into this story?

- The friends can't carry the paralytic through the front door, so they go through the roof instead. What might be an example of "coming to Jesus through the roof" (i.e., in a creative, unexpected way)?

Pray It Forward 🙏

Do you know anyone who could use some determined, creative "mat-carrying" from a friend or two? Present that person to Jesus in prayer together.

Jesus, we carry _____ to you and lower him/her into your presence right now. We believe in you as the One who can turn lives around. Please do all that you need to do for his/her forgiveness and healing. Amen.

DAY 3:
HOW NOT TO HELP
Week 5: HOW CAN I HELP?

There's no one in *Because of Grácia* to use as an example of this next role—not even Bobbi's poor preoccupied dad. Perhaps we could point to the people at his church who are "breathing down his neck," but we still don't know for sure.

That role is the thankful Pharisee. It may sound unusual, but it's not actually as rare as one might hope. It's a role people are easily tempted to play when situations like teen pregnancy occur.

Listen to this parable of Jesus, which illustrates what we're talking about.

Read the Word

One conversation partner can read the voice of the narrator and Jesus, and the other can read the voices of the two characters.

To some who were confident of their own righteousness and looked down on everybody else, Jesus told this parable: "Two men went up to the temple to pray, one a Pharisee and the other a tax collector. The Pharisee stood by himself and prayed: 'God, I thank you that I am not like other people—robbers, evildoers, adulterers—or even like this tax collector. I fast twice a week and give a tenth of all I get.'

"But the tax collector stood at a distance. He would not even look up to heaven, but beat his breast and said, 'God, have mercy on me, a sinner.'

"I tell you that this man, rather than the other, went home justified before God. For all those who exalt themselves will be humbled, and those who humble themselves will be exalted."
Luke 18:9–14

Think It Over

A few words about Pharisees before we discuss the parable. We tend to think of them as obvious bad guys, since that is what the name Pharisee has come to mean. In Jesus's time, it was just the opposite. Pharisees were admired as the people trying their very hardest to do what was right. Paul described them as "the strictest sect of our religion" (Acts 26:5). And he would know, because he was one himself, faultless in rule-based righteousness (Philippians 3:5–6)

Problem is, Jesus was introducing a new kind of righteousness, located not so much in rules as in the overall attitude of the heart. This righteousness of the kingdom of God would still pursue the good things promoted by the rules, but it would go even further, humbly empowered by God.

Back to the parable. Our first clue that something is off is when the first character stands up and starts praying about himself. He thanks God that he is not like other people and that he is so earnest and successful in doing the right things. Meanwhile, the other man, a despised tax collector, can't even lift his head. All he can pray is, "God, have mercy on me. I'm getting it so very wrong."

Jesus said it was the second man whom God considered righteous at the end of the day.

Talk It Over

- In what way would it be tempting to play the role of a thankful Pharisee in relation to young people who had fooled around and gotten pregnant?

- Is it possible to do your best to live the right way and not look down on others at the same time? How does one strike that balance?

- In what way would it be tempting to play the role of the thankful Pharisee in relation to someone who had had an abortion?

Tell It Over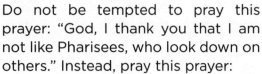

Take a few minutes to rewrite the Parable of the Pharisee and the Tax Collector for a modern-day setting. Replace the characters and their actions with new ones that communicate the same message for our time and place. Who are the "best" people? What are the good things they do? Who are the "worst" people?

Pray It Forward

Do not be tempted to pray this prayer: "God, I thank you that I am not like Pharisees, who look down on others." Instead, pray this prayer:

God, thank you for your amazing grace, which so mercifully takes who I am—a person who sometimes does the right thing, sometimes does the wrong thing, and sometimes can't tell the difference—and forms me into the image of your Son. Forgive me for the times I have looked down on others or resented the mercy you show to sinners. Bring all of us sinners safely home to your love, through our Lord and Savior Jesus Christ. Amen.

DAY 4:
EGYPTIAN CIVIL DISOBEDIENCE
Week 6: HOW CAN I HELP?

Okay, here's a thorny one. What would Grace, Chase, and OB have done if they hadn't met Bobbi outside the abortion clinic? Would they have gone inside and tried to find her? Would they have crossed boundaries and pursued her right into a prep room or beyond? The whole situation could have become very messy.

In such a situation, it would have been very important to keep Bobbi's dignity and freedom intact. And if the three friends had broken any rule of the clinic, they would have needed to be fully prepared to accept the consequences.

Thankfully, the crisis with Bobbi never reaches that point. The rescue takes place in her own heart, where the Spirit of God whispers, "Stop."

This guidebook does not recommend civil disobedience (that is, breaking the laws of the land in service of a higher ideal) regarding the issue of abortion. But we do want to take a look at a fascinating Old Testament story that gives an example of civil disobedience's appropriate use: the story of the ancient Egyptian midwives, Shiphrah and Puah.

Read the Word 📖

Now Joseph and all his brothers and all that generation died, but the Israelites were exceedingly fruitful; they multiplied greatly, increased in numbers and became so numerous that the land was filled with them.

Then a new king, to whom Joseph meant nothing, came to power in Egypt. "Look," he said to his people, "the Israelites have become far too numerous for us. Come, we must deal shrewdly with them or they will become even more numerous and, if war breaks out, will join our enemies, fight against us and leave the country."

So they put slave masters over them to oppress them with forced labor.

This didn't work, and the Israelites multiplied even more.

The king of Egypt said to the Hebrew midwives, whose names were Shiphrah and Puah, "When you are helping the Hebrew women during childbirth on the delivery stool, if you see that the baby is a boy, kill him; but if it is a girl, let her live. The midwives, however, feared God and did not do what the king of Egypt had told them to do; they let the boys live. Then the king of Egypt summoned the midwives and asked them, "Why have you done this? Why have you let the boys live?"

The midwives answered Pharaoh, "Hebrew women are not like Egyptian women; they are vigorous and give birth before the midwives arrive."
So God was kind to the midwives and the people increased and became even more numerous. And because the midwives feared God, he gave them families of their own.

Then Pharaoh gave this order to all his people: "Every Hebrew boy that is born you must throw into the Nile, but let every girl live."
Exodus 1:6–11, 15–22

Talk It Over

- What do you think? Just like with King Herod's slaughter of the innocents in Bethlehem, is this another large leap to get from a Bible story to our present-day situation? Or isn't it?

- Why did Shiphrah and Puah take the risk of disobeying their ruler?

- Ponder for a minute. Is there anyone in our own society who could play the same kind of game-changing role these Egyptian midwives did?

Think It Over 💬

Sex-selective abortion is an ongoing problem in our world. That's when parents find out a child's sex ahead of time, through ultrasound and other technologies, and abort it if it isn't the sex they want. The United Nations Population Fund estimates that 117 million women are missing from Asia and Eastern Europe due to the practice because their lives were aborted. In some places, it has become difficult for many men to find a woman to marry because the gender ratio is so unbalanced.

Pray It Forward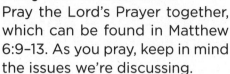

Pray the Lord's Prayer together, which can be found in Matthew 6:9–13. As you pray, keep in mind the issues we're discussing.

Try It Out ✔

Considering the destitute, Proverbs says, "Speak up for those who cannot speak for themselves" (Proverbs 31:8). Regarding victims of injustice, it says, "Rescue those being led away to death; hold back those staggering toward slaughter. If you say, 'But we knew nothing about this,' does not he who weighs the heart perceive it?" (Proverbs 24:11–12). These texts were not written specifically about unborn children, but we can use them to outline a general pattern of righteous action regarding vulnerable people.

What kind of action might that suggest regarding the present-day situation of abortion? It might mean writing a letter to a government representative expressing your views. It might mean learning statistics and sharing them with others. It might even mean joining a prayer vigil near an abortion clinic or taking training to provide compassionate pro-life sidewalk counseling.

That's a lot to try out, isn't it? May God call you, lead you, and bless you in your willingness to learn.

DAY 5:
DELIVER US FROM EVIL
Week 6: HOW CAN I HELP?

In the previous entry, we ruled out breaking the law as a means of addressing the moral crisis of abortion in our society. There are people out there who have committed violent crimes against abortion facilities and doctors, viewing themselves as freewheeling warriors in a battle of good against evil. But attacking one wrong with another leads to moral and spiritual absurdity. Even more, such destructive actions against specific people and places fail to understand the true enemy we face.

Think of the doctor Bobbi sees for her pregnancy test, who provides her with information about the abortion clinic. You may not have liked this doctor's manner, but she is not the sworn enemy of life, God, and the unborn. She is just another flesh-and-blood human being with her own story, caught up unwittingly in a larger struggle. What might that story be? Did you wonder, when she turns away as Bobbi begins to cry? What has this doctor seen and experienced and suffered in her life?

We don't usually know exactly where our moral "opponents" are coming from, especially if we don't take the chance to sit down with them as people and find out. But we do know that they are loved by God no matter what, and that they are souls on a journey the same as we are. The struggle to persuade a person's conscience against the practice of abortion is not a vicious fight to the death with those who practice it, but a prayerful fight against the overarching idea and pattern of evil.

Read the Word

Read this passage with your conversation partner, taking turns each sentence.

For our struggle is not against flesh and blood, but against the rulers, against the authorities, against the powers of this dark world and against the spiritual forces of evil in the heavenly realms. Therefore put on the full armor of God, so that when the day of evil comes, you may be able to stand your ground, and after you have done everything, to stand. Stand firm then, with the belt of truth buckled around your waist, with the breastplate of righteousness in place, and with your feet fitted with the readiness that comes from the gospel of peace. In addition to all this, take up the shield of faith, with which you can extinguish all the flaming arrows of the evil one. Take the helmet of salvation and the sword of the Spirit, which is the word of God. And pray in the Spirit on all occasions with all kinds of prayers and requests.
Ephesians 6:12–18

Play It Over ▶

Test each other's memory of the passage with a game of speed charades. One person mimes pieces of armor or equipment, in any particular order, and the other person names what they represent. See how long it takes you to get 5 right answers.

Talk It Over 💬

- How do you picture the "spiritual forces of evil"?

- Which of the pieces of equipment named in the passage do you feel you need the most in your life?

- Are there situations and issues in which it doesn't make sense to pray? Are there prayers and requests that God isn't interested in hearing? (Check the passage again to make sure.)

Ask A Mentor ❓

Ask a trusted adult which piece of the armor of God has been most important for them in their life. If they can't think of one offhand, read the passage with them.

Pray It Forward 🙏

"And pray in the Spirit on all occasions," says Ephesians 6:18. Try that in the days ahead.

Lord, I open my heart for you to blow through like a rushing wind, stirring up the prayers you want me to pray on this issue of "Choosing Life." I open my mouth to speak all the words of worship, confession, intercession, and blessing that you set on fire within me by your Spirit, through Jesus Christ. Amen.

VOICING FAITH

CONVERSATION 1

WHY DO WE HIDE?

THE DYNAMICS OF
UNDERCOVER CHRISTIANITY

GROUP SESSION

From Jesus's right hand man Peter, who sometimes acts before thinking, to Chase Morgan, who avoids conflict at all costs and never speaks up, Christians have often been tempted to pretend in public that they aren't followers of Jesus. What is that all about? In this session we take a sympathetic look at our fear of other people's opinions and point to the forgiveness and fresh start provided by the Lord we love.

 **REEL to REAL**

1. Undercover man

- Why do you think Chase has decided he can't make a difference in his world?

- Are guys more likely to hide their faith than girls, or is it an equal temptation for everyone?

- How might someone complete this sentence? "I hide the fact that I'm a Christian because. . . "

- Chase says he isn't worried about thriving in high school; he's just trying to survive. What are the keys to "surviving" high school, in your opinion?

- How is being an undercover Christian similar to being an undercover policeman? How is it different?

2. Are you a Christian, Chase?

- Why does Chase answer "no" at first?

- Why do you think he changes his answer?

- What does it feel like to worry about other people's opinions of us?

3. Grace on the hot seat

- How would you describe Mr. Livingston's attitude toward Grace in this scene? What's up with that?

- Even though she knows a lot about the subject, Grace isn't keen to share her view on the origin of life in front of the class. Why not?

- What gets her to the point of agreeing to talk about it?

4. Most influential person of all time

• Can you relate to this scene? Have you ever been in a situation like this?

• How is Chase feeling as people in the class begin proposing answers to Mr. B's question?

• What is Chase's daydream all about? Do you think it gets him closer to taking action or pushes him further away from it?

• How easy or difficult would it be to suggest that Jesus is the most influential person of all time?

• What are some words to describe how Chase feels at the end of the scene?

ENGAGE THE WORD

1 **Matthew 26: Peter denies Jesus**

- Why do you think this story is included in all 4 Gospels?

- All the disciples insisted that they would never disown Jesus. How did that change so quickly?

- Describe the rest of this night as you imagine it for Peter.

- What do you think was the worst part of it for Peter: remembering words like "he who disowns me" or knowing he had let his friend down?

2 **John 21:1–19: Jesus reinstates Peter**

- Why did Peter jump in the water when he realized it was Jesus on the shore?

- Why do you think Jesus cooks them breakfast before having a conversation with Peter?

- What is that conversation about? Why does Jesus ask Peter the same question 3 times? What exactly is he asking Peter to do for him?

- What do you think of Jesus's final challenge to Peter to "Follow me"?

- Do you think Jesus will disown Peter before the angels of God one day, or has Peter been forgiven? If so, when exactly did that forgiveness occur? Did Peter have to earn it?

- Have you ever pretended you didn't know Jesus?

CARRY IT OUT
The Persecuted Church

Look up some information about a persecuted Christian community in one of the following places, past or present: China, the former Soviet Union, India, Ethiopia, Vietnam, Indonesia, Turkey, Pakistan, Sudan, or the Middle-Eastern territory controlled by Daesh (ISIS). As you share what you've learned with others around you, explore these questions:

- What kind of persecution happened, or is happening, and how has it affected the church in that place?

- How have other Christians helped their persecuted brothers and sisters in this place?

- How should we pray for this group?

If the persecution is ongoing, consider writing a letter of advocacy to regional or international government representatives expressing your concern about it. Or perhaps choose this group or historical situation for an in-depth research project at school.

DAY 1:
I COULDN'T SAY IT
Week 7: WHY DO WE HIDE?

"Today in history, Mr. B asked us who was the most influential person in the world, and I knew the answer. I even wrote it down . . . I just . . . I couldn't say it. It was like I was paralyzed."

Chase is talking at the campfire about the latest episode in his ongoing saga of undercover faith. He has had enough of it. Keeping silent leaves him depressed and disgusted with himself. How will he ever get beyond this problem? The daydreams in which he tries out life ahead of time only leave him frozen when faced with reality. Something has to change.

Thankfully Chase has Grace in his life, who is willing to listen sympathetically and encourage rather than add to the condemnation he's been heaping on himself. "Chase," she says, "you might not see this, but there's something inside of you that's so inspiring."

No, he doesn't see it yet. But her words offer the glimmer of a new possibility. Maybe there is a way forward for him after all.

That way arises soon through Grace's own example. When she shares a story about her past that she might have reason to be ashamed of, she becomes a model for Chase of what it looks like to open up to others. Her demonstration jump-starts his own poetic storytelling, which then makes the leap from campfire to classroom.

Read the Word 📖

Read through the following passages with your conversation partner.

*Have I not commanded you? Be strong and courageous. Do not be afraid; do not be discouraged, for the L*ORD *your God will be with you wherever you go.*
Joshua 1:9

So do not fear, for I am with you; do not be dismayed, for I am your God. I will strengthen you and help you; I will uphold you with my righteous right hand.
Isaiah 41:10

For the Spirit God gave us does not make us timid, but gives us power, love and self-discipline.
2 Timothy 1:7

Surely I am with you always, to the very end of the age.
Matthew 28:20

Perhaps Chase finds courage to take the plunge by following the example of Jesus himself. Jesus didn't seek rejection for its own sake, but in his loving resolve to carry the sorrows of the world, he was willing to be despised if necessary.

I did not hide my face from mocking and spitting. Because the Sovereign L*ORD* *helps me, I will not be disgraced. Therefore have I set my face like flint, and I know I will not be put to shame. He who vindicates me is near.*
Isaiah 50:6–8

Now Jesus instills his own courage into our hearts through the Spirit he has given us.

Pray It Forward 🙏

Lord, you know all things. You know just what my heart needs in order to grow in courage. Speak your word of reassurance to me today. I believe you are with me to the end. Amen.

Talk It Over 💬

- Why do God and his representatives have to tell people so often not to be afraid?

- What is the main reason not to fear that's given by today's verses?

- Who is someone you know who is an inspiring example of courage to you?

DAY 2:
FEAR OF MAN, FEAR OF GOD
Week 7: WHY DO WE HIDE?

Before Chase starts drawing encouragement from Grácia to let his Christian identity be known, there's an occasion where she inadvertently makes him want to hide it. You know the one I'm talking about: that first phone call.

"Chase, are you a Christian?" Grácia asks.

"Well, no . . ."

"You're not?"

"No, no—what I meant to say is, nobody's ever really asked me that before."

"So you are a Christian?"

"Yes. But I'm not a fanatic or anything like that."

This is a really funny scene, since Chase's embarrassment is so common and easy to relate to. There's a spiritual name for what he's suffering. We often call it "the fear of man." "Fear of man will prove to be a snare," says Proverbs 29:25, "but whoever trusts in the Lord is kept safe." This isn't talking about fear of men in a literal sense. "Fear of man" means worrying too much about what other people think, and shaping your actions and choices by that fear.

Remember the character of Amy in the film? She seems to be stifled by the same fear in her life, as she sometimes expresses her enthusiasm for the perspective of faith and truth but then has to silence herself once more to keep Josie happy. Amy's concern about her friends' opinions of her eventually moves her to agree to do something that goes against her own heart: fake a prayer request in order to trap Mr. Brady.

Getting back to Chase, his "fear of man" has to do with the opinion of a girl he admires. He wonders, *What will she think of me if she finds out I'm a Christian?*

Will she reject me completely? Even after he's admitted the fact that he's a Christian, he is quick to clarify that he's not a "fanatic." Chase wants to be liked, frankly. Don't we all?

Read the Word

Not to pick on the Apostle Peter too much here, especially after our last group lesson, but a certain situation in Galatians shows how the fear of man that attacked Peter during Jesus's arrest and trial took a little longer to be rooted out of his life completely. Even in his new role as a Spirit-empowered missionary for Christ, Peter was not yet immune to the powerful desire to be liked by others.

When Cephas [Peter] came to Antioch, I opposed him to his face, because he stood condemned [i.e., he was clearly in the wrong]. For before certain men came from James, he used to eat with Gentiles. But when they arrived, he began to draw back and separate himself from the Gentiles because he was afraid of those who belonged to the circumcision group. The other Jews joined him in his hypocrisy, so that by their hypocrisy even Barnabas was led astray.

When I saw that they were not acting in line with the truth of the gospel, I said to Cephas [Peter] in front of them all, "You are a Jew, yet you live like a Gentile and not like a Jew. How is it, then, that you force Gentiles to follow Jewish customs?

"We who are Jews by birth and not sinful Gentiles know that a person is not justified by the works of the law, but by faith in Jesus Christ."
Galatians 2:11–16

The issue here had to do with a group called the "Judaizers" who were travelling around to Gentile churches telling people that they had to obey Jewish law if they wanted to be Christians. Paul opposed them fiercely, since he had come to know Jesus as the one who gives new life by his own merciful grace, not because of religious hoops we jump through (Titus 3:4–6).

Peter had learned this too (Acts 10). But the peer pressure of some religious visitors caused him to "forget" it temporarily—to deny

Jesus one more time and pretend that Gentiles were a spiritual lower class. Peter didn't want to be criticized or rejected by the visitors for associating openly with the Gentiles.

So Paul called him on it. Paul knew all about this kind of religious pressure. He had long ago rejected it: "If I were still trying to please people, I would not be a servant of Christ!" he said (Galatians 1:10).

Talk It Over

- Fear of man can make Christians hide from the big, bad world out there. Fear can also make them hide from other Christians. Have you ever seen this in your own experience?

- Is there any area of life in particular where you are struggling with the fear of man?

Pray It Forward

Pray together about that area.

DAY 3:
GOD DOESN'T USE PEOPLE LIKE US
Week 7: WHY DO WE HIDE?

Remember that special conversation by the fire when Grace tells Chase there is something inspiring inside him? You might remember that OB was less than supportive in that moment. He laughed at the idea of God using people like him and Chase.

"The guv'ner? Ha! That's a good one. Grace, you crack me up."

"That wasn't supposed to be funny," she replies. OB explains himself further.

"Listen, God doesn't use people like me and him—no offense, Guv'ner. He uses people like you. You're so *together*."

She has to set him straight after that.

We realize in this scene that there are different ways of being undercover as a Christian. There is "undercover" in the sense of the secret agent trying to do his job but not wanting to be recognized by anyone as he goes about it. And there's "undercover" in the sense of being covered up and covered over by the lie that you are not virtuous or spiritual enough to be used by God. This kind of "undercover Christian" thinks, *Action belongs to others, not to me.*

There are two problems with this attitude. First, it sells you short and smothers the glory God kindles within you. Secondly, it disses God. Who are we to say what he can or can't do, whom he can or can't use?

Read the Word 📖

God has worked with many unlikely candidates in his time, with many younger brothers and weaker tribes. When it came time to anoint a king for Israel from the family of Jesse, God gave Samuel an important warning:

The Lord does not look at the things people look at. People look at the outward appearance, but the Lord looks at the heart.
1 Samuel 16:7

The only thing really required for God to use us is our willingness to be used. He has placed his light in us. We have to let it shine, as Jesus said:

"You are the light of the world. A town built on a hill cannot be hidden. Neither do people light a lamp and put it under a bowl. Instead they put it on its stand, and it gives light to everyone in the house. In the same way, let your light shine before others, that they may see your good deeds and glorify your Father in heaven."
Matthew 5:14–16

That image gives a whole new flavor to the word *undercover*. A light is not made to be covered up. A light is made to shine.

Listen Up 🎧

Go online and find the most high-energy version of "This Little Light of Mine" that you can. Sing along. Share the link with your conversation partner.

Talk It Over 💬

• If you've ever been an undercover Christian, what kind of "undercover" was it?

• Does God use people like you?

• With this talk of power in weakness, what ideas come to mind of something God could do through you?

Pray It Forward 🙏

Dear God, when I presume you cannot use me, forgive me for thinking so little of you. I know that your light can shine from me and accomplish all that you desire. Here's my heart again, to receive your will and reflect the grace of Jesus.

DAY 4:
BLESSED WHEN INSULTED
Week 7: WHY DO WE HIDE?

Sometimes the world will not welcome the light—neither the Light of the World, Jesus, nor the light shining from his followers. "This is the verdict," writes John. "Light has come into the world, but people loved darkness instead of light because their deeds were evil. Everyone who does evil hates the light" (John 3:19–20).

That's the very thing we're afraid of when, like Chase, we're afraid to speak up as Christians—right? We fear rejection, ridicule, hatred, or worse. Floating around in our minds may be some New Testament words about rejoicing in persecution or something like that, but we figure they must apply to crazy, radical, *fanatical* Christians, not to people like us. Our problems are minor ones: a bit of mockery, a bit of name-calling, occasional gossip. How do we deal with this subtle brand of modern-day persecution, if it can even be called that anymore?

Well, maybe we should take another look at those New Testament passages. Maybe they've got more to say to us than we expect.

Read the Word

Take turns reading these scriptures to each other.

Dear friends, do not be surprised at the fiery ordeal that has come on you to test you, as though something strange were happening to you. But rejoice inasmuch as you participate in the sufferings of Christ, so that you may be overjoyed when his glory is revealed. If you are insulted because of the name of Christ, you are blessed, for the Spirit of glory and of God rests on you. If you suffer, it should not be as a murderer or thief or any other kind of criminal, or even as a meddler. However, if you suffer as a Christian, do not be ashamed, but praise God that you bear that name.
1 Peter 4:12–16

"Blessed are those who are persecuted because of righteousness, for theirs is the kingdom of heaven. Blessed are you when people insult you, persecute you and falsely say all kinds of evil against you because of me. Rejoice and be glad, because great is your reward in heaven, for in the same way they persecuted the prophets who were before you."
Matthew 5:10–12

Think It Over

Do you notice how verbal forms of persecution are front and center in these passages? These words are not only about some long-ago time when religion was a rougher business. They speak to our day and age too, and to the subtle (or not-so-subtle) opposition Christians may experience.

Do you notice something else about these passages? The first one was written by Peter—yes, the same Peter who disowned Jesus and got a little intimidated by the "popular people" of the faith in Antioch.

Peter became the rock on which the church was built. He knew his stuff when it came to persecution. He was part of a Spirit-crazy group that was flogged by the Sanhedrin one day for preaching in the temple courts. The book of Acts says that they left the place "rejoicing because they had been counted worthy of suffering disgrace for the Name" (Acts 5:41).

Talk It Over

- What is the worst thing that has ever happened to you because you were a Christian?

- What is the worst thing you could imagine happening to you because you are a Christian?

- Seemingly with a twinkle in his eye, Jesus said to his disciples, "Truly I tell you. . . no one who has left home or brothers or sisters or mother or father or children or fields for me and the gospel will fail to receive a hundred times as much in this present age: homes, brothers, sisters, mothers, children and fields—along with persecutions—and in the age to come eternal life" (Mark 10:29–30). Why do you think he included persecution in this list of blessings?

Ask A Mentor

Ask a Christian adult you know if they have ever experienced persecution. How long did it last? What did they do about it? What did God do about it?

Pray It Forward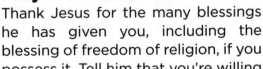

Thank Jesus for the many blessings he has given you, including the blessing of freedom of religion, if you possess it. Tell him that you're willing to be insulted because of his name, if it means knowing that name better and better making it known.

DAY 5:
NECESSARY HIDING
Week 7: WHY DO WE HIDE?

Psalm 34 has an interesting subtitle: "Of David. When he pretended to be insane before Abimelek, who drove him away, and he left." If we turn to 1 Samuel 21, we can read the whole story.

Read the Word 📖

That day David fled from Saul and went to Achish king of Gath. But the servants of Achish said to him, "Isn't this David, the king of the land? Isn't he the one they sing about in their dances: 'Saul has slain his thousands, and David his tens of thousands'?"

David took these words to heart and was very much afraid of Achish king of Gath. So he pretended to be insane in their presence; and while he was in their hands he acted like a madman, making marks on the doors of the gate and letting saliva run down his beard.

Achish said to his servants, "Look at the man! He is insane! Why bring him to me? Am I so short of madmen that you have to bring this fellow here to carry on like this in front of me? Must this man come into my house?"
1 Samuel 21:10–15

David was hiding. For a little while he was an undercover king—not because he was ashamed or feared insult, but because he needed to protect his own life.

The apostle Paul was in similar situations many times. At least twice, he had to be smuggled out of a city by being lowered in a basket through an opening in the wall (Acts 9:25; 2 Corinthians 11:33).

Jesus had to hide himself when people wanted to make him king by force or seize him before his time (John 6:15; 10:39). Both Jesus and Moses had to be hidden as children from kings who wanted to kill them (Matthew 2; Exodus 2). And the Christians in Jerusalem had to run away across the whole region when a great persecution broke out against them following the stoning of Stephen (Acts 8:1).

Think It Over

This is the "hiding" situation of many Christians in our world. It's not insult they fear so much as injury and death. These Christians don't fear getting body-checked in the school hallway—like what happened to Grace—as much as getting their house or church burned down, possibly with them inside it.

In parts of the world, it is illegal to convert to another faith aside from the faith of the land. Members of your own family might think you deserve death for conversion. In such places Christians live underground as a way of life.

Paradoxically, the church often grows during times of threat and suppression. But such a way of life takes its toll. No one would ask to suffer in this way. We should remember to pray for the persecuted Christians in places like India, China, and Iraq.

Learning about their experiences both challenges us to keep our own struggles in perspective and encourages us to make good use of the freedom of religion we have in the West. One use we may make of it is to advocate for those who lack such freedom.

Talk It Over

- Would you consider it persecution when Josie bumps Grace in the hall?

- Would you consider it persecution when Josie, Zabrina, and Amy make a video of Mr. Brady praying, with malicious intent?

- Would you consider it persecution when Mr. Livingston argues against Grace's views about divine creation?

- Would you consider it persecution when Mr. Brady is suspended from his job for breaking a school rule and praying with a student?

Pray It Forward

Considering his love, power, and creativity, God can use even persecution to fulfill his good purposes. When the Jerusalem Christians were scattered throughout Judea and Samaria, they carried the message of new life with them as they went, and the good news of Jesus spread throughout the region.

Pray for our world, that the word of hope would spread even more in the places where Christians are under pressure. And pray for readiness to be a witness yourself.

CONVERSATION 2

WHAT IS A WITNESS?

*TELLING OUR STORIES
AS CHRISTIANS*

GROUP SESSION

Thanks to encouragement from friends and a good example to imitate, Chase moves from sheepish silence to bold public expression of his personal faith experience. He takes the risk of telling what he knows, with the added vulnerability and power of using an artistic skill to do so. We underestimate the influence this kind of heartfelt expression can have on our peers. Chase is an inspiration to all of us.

 **REEL to REAL**

1. **Chase's spoken word (first viewing)**

- At the campfire, what is the effect on Chase when Grace tells the story of her negative relationship in California?

- How do you think we get from campfire performance to classroom performance? Why does Chase decide to take such a risk and how does he prepare himself?

- What are the risks of doing what Chase does?

- How do his classmates actually respond? Does their response surprise you?

- Would you ever do something like this? Why or why not?

2. Chase's spoken word (second viewing)

- What individual words and phrases stuck in your mind this time through? What did you find powerful? Did anything strike a chord with you?

- What is Chase doing more of in this poem: telling people what they should believe, or telling them what he believes? What's the difference?

ENGAGE THE WORD

Today's scripture is Acts 25:23–26:29

- What is the basis of Paul's defense?

- If you were King Agrippa, would you find it convincing?

- What is the most effective aspect of a testimony about personal experience?

- Is there a negative aspect?

- Which aspect do you think is stronger?

DAY 1:
I'M NOT MAKING THIS UP
Week 8: WHAT IS A WITNESS?

Chase is a dreamer. He makes up stories in his head in which he is the hero. Not such a bad trait to have, really. It shows a certain optimism. But his daydreaming becomes a problem when it pulls him out of the real situation in front of him and forestalls all that he might contribute to that situation in the flesh.

Chase's habit would probably make him a good storyteller or filmmaker—but possibly not the best witness in a court of law. Imagine a lawyer asking him, "What really happened that day, when the crime took place?" Would Chase ever start confusing his daydreams with reality?

Christians have been accused of that kind of thing before. The first people to hear the stories of Jesus's empty tomb, stories of a mysterious gardener with scarred wrists and a figure who moved through locked doors, probably wondered if the storytellers were "seeing things." They may have presumed that the first witnesses to Christ's resurrection were just victims of wishful thinking. Maybe that's why the generation who lived with Jesus in the flesh before and after the resurrection later made such a point to emphasize the reality of what they had experienced.

Read the Word

Read the following scripture passages aloud.

That which was from the beginning, which we have heard, which we have seen with our eyes, which we have looked at and our hands have touched—this we proclaim concerning the Word of life. The life appeared; we have seen it and testify to it, and we proclaim to you the eternal life, which was with the Father and has appeared to us. We proclaim to you what we have seen and heard, so that you also may have fellowship with us.
1 John 1:1–3

John wrote about Jesus in a poetic way. Some people were denying that Jesus had been a man with a regular physical body, but John knew that such an idea would endanger the real-life character of Jesus's death and resurrection. He knew Jesus was divine while also fully human.

In his older age, the apostle Peter made a different point.

We did not follow cleverly devised stories when we told you about the coming of our Lord Jesus Christ in power, but we were eyewitnesses of his majesty. He received honor and glory from God the Father when the voice came to him from the Majestic Glory, saying, "This is my Son, whom I love; with him I am well pleased." We ourselves heard this voice that came from heaven when we were with him on the sacred mountain.
2 Peter 1:16–18

Peter was remembering the time he, James, and John climbed a mountain with Jesus and watched him transfigure into dazzling white before their eyes, while a cloud surrounded them and a heavenly voice spoke. Almost sounds like a Chase-style daydream, doesn't it?

The experience ended as abruptly as it had begun, and the four walked back down the mountain. Jesus ordered them not to tell anyone about it until after he had risen from the dead. They couldn't figure out what he meant at the time. In his later life, Peter put all the pieces together. Yes, Jesus was human, but Jesus was also truly divine.

With their own particular emphases, Peter and John were both telling the next generation, "We're not making this up. This really did happen."

Think It Over 💬

It's the basic pattern of all Christian witness. We're not called to tell what we think should have happened, or what sounds good, or what will be the most agreeable to our listeners' worldviews. We are called to tell what we know for ourselves about Jesus—the tangible stuff that has taken place in our lives as a result of following him. If we've mainly been riding on the ideas and experiences of others in our journey of Christian faith, we may need to begin making our faith our own in a concrete way.

We live in a culture that is very interested in the real-life experiences of the individual. Our culture is even willing to push back against established fact in order to honor the individual's unique perspective. While we may not get very far with people by saying, "This is the truth and you had better believe it," we may find a sympathetic audience when we humbly say, "This is what I have experienced and it has made all the difference for me." Such an approach doesn't give up on the idea of absolute truth. It just speaks a language of personal truth that our culture can actually hear.

That's what happens in Chase's history class when he gets up one day and shares in vulnerable, poetic form about who Jesus is for him personally. Telling a personal story is the biggest kind of risk a person can take—a risk that is respected and admired in our culture, as we see in Chase's classmates' response.

Talk It Over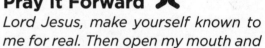

- Do you ever daydream? What about?

- What's a story from your own experience that illustrates who Jesus is and how he helps and changes us?

Try It Out ✔

Watch for a natural opportunity to tell your "Talk It Over" story to another person—either a believer, a nonbeliever, or someone in between.

Pray It Forward 🙏

Lord Jesus, make yourself known to me for real. Then open my mouth and heart so I may share what I know.

DAY 2:
ONE THING I DO KNOW
Week 8: WHAT IS A WITNESS?

We've all heard the song "Amazing Grace" at some point or another. We may have heard it and sung it so often, in fact, that we don't really think about what it says anymore.

This famous song was written by an ex-captain of slave-trading ships in England—which may explain his choice of the word wretch to refer to himself. But some of the most familiar words in that first verse of John Newton's song come from a Bible story about a controversial healing Jesus performed in Jerusalem.

Read the Word

Take turns reading each time a new paragraph begins.

As he went along, he saw a man blind from birth. His disciples asked him, "Rabbi, who sinned, this man or his parents, that he was born blind?"

"Neither this man nor his parents sinned," said Jesus, "but this happened so that the works of God might be displayed in him". . .

He spat on the ground, made some mud with the saliva, and put it on the man's eyes. "Go," he told him, "wash in the Pool of Siloam" (this word means "sent"). So the man went and washed, and came home seeing.

His neighbors and those who had formerly seen him begging asked, "Isn't this the same man who used to sit and beg?" Some claimed that he was.

Others said, "No, he only looks like him."

But he himself insisted, "I am the man."

"How then were your eyes opened?" they asked.

He replied, "The man they call Jesus made some mud and put it on my eyes. He told me to go to Siloam and wash. So I went and washed, and then I could see."
"Where is this man?" they asked him.

"I don't know," he said.
John 9:1–3; 6–12

Let's take note of a couple of things. First, consider how concrete details like saliva and mud bring this story to life. It's good to include vivid details when describing real-life experience with the Lord. Second, consider how people definitely notice, but don't always believe the explanation of, real-life transformation in others.

The story goes on from here with the religious officials investigating what has happened. They're upset because the healing has taken place on the Sabbath day, when no one is supposed to work according to Jewish law. (Jesus made mud, which would've been considered "work.") They decide that Jesus is not from God since he breaks the law. At the same time, how is he able to perform a miracle? So the controversy continues.

Meanwhile, the man who has been healed sticks to what he knows, retelling the story of what happened to him. When they keep pressing him, he eventually says the words John Newton uses in his song: "One thing I do know. I was blind but now I see!" (John 9:25).

Talk It Over 💬

- Why do the disciples ask about sin at the beginning of the story?

- What do you think of Jesus's reply to them?

- Like Newton, Grácia says, "I've experienced God's grace in a way I can't explain." How would you begin describing grace—both what it means, and how it has changed your life?

Listen Up 🎧

If you aren't too shy, sing the first verse of "Amazing Grace" out loud together. Here are the lyrics:

Amazing grace,
How sweet the sound
That saved a wretch like me
I once was lost,
But now am found
Was blind, but now I see

If you are too shy, find a version of someone singing it online and hum along.

After you sing, think of this: John Newton wrote this song to put the work of God in his life on display. "Amazing Grace" has preserved the memory of his conversion for nearly 250 years, for the benefit of millions and millions of people.

Pray It Forward 🙏

God, put your work on display in my life.

DAY 3:
GO HOME TO YOUR FAMILY
Week 8: WHAT IS A WITNESS?

You'd think Jesus was trying to keep himself secret half the time. In the Gospels of Matthew, Mark, and Luke, a strange thing happens over and over: Jesus heals someone and then promptly orders them not to tell anyone about it. It happens so often that you'll easily find examples when you read the Gospels. (Look up Mark 1:40–45 to see one.)

John's Gospel is a little different than the others, but even that one begins with a secret miracle: Jesus turning water into wine in a back room where only the kitchen workers know about it.

What's all this secrecy about? Lots of ink has been spilled to explain the "Messianic Secret"—the way Jesus tries to keep his true identity hidden as he carries on his ministry in Israel. Maybe Jesus was trying to avoid creating a mass movement that would get carried away with miracles and lose the Giver in the gifts. Maybe he was trying to delay his ultimate confrontation with the religious authorities. Or maybe he was just using reverse psychology, expecting people would do the exact opposite of what he said!

Whatever the case, we're going to look today at a counterexample to the Messianic Secret: the healing of a demon-possessed man in the Gentile-majority area of the Gerasenes. It's one of the few times before the resurrection when Jesus explicitly tells someone to go and share with others exactly what they have experienced with him.

Read the Word

They went across the lake to the region of the Gerasenes. When Jesus got out of the boat, a man with an impure spirit came from the tombs to meet him. This man lived in the tombs, and no one could bind him anymore, not even with a chain. For he had often been chained hand and foot, but he tore the chains apart and broke the irons on his feet. No one was strong enough to subdue him. Night and day among the tombs and in the hills he would cry out and cut himself with stones.

When he saw Jesus from a distance, he ran and fell on his knees in front of him.
Mark 5:1–5

This man would have been an unnerving sight, to say the least. But Jesus had things under control. He spoke calmly, ordered the legion of demons to leave the man, and let them enter a nearby herd of two thousand pigs. The pigs, for their part, promptly ran down the bank into the lake and drowned. The pandemonium in the water must have been horrific.

Meanwhile, the people tending the pigs ran away and told what had happened, and the people of the area began pleading with Jesus to leave their region. He was messing with the status quo just a little too much.

Then this happened:

As Jesus was getting into the boat, the man who had been demon-possessed begged to go with him. Jesus did not let him, but said, "Go home to your own people and tell them how much the Lord has done for you, and how he has had mercy on you." So the man went away and began to tell in the Decapolis how much Jesus had done for him. And all the people were amazed.
Mark 5:18–20

Talk It Over 💬

- If you were miraculously healed by Jesus, would you be able to keep it a secret? If not, whom would you tell first?

- Why do you think the healed demoniac wanted to go along with Jesus?

- Why do you think Jesus told him to go home instead?

Pray It Forward 🙏

In the book of Acts, the religious leaders in Jerusalem order Peter and John not to speak publicly in the name of Jesus anymore. Peter and John reply that it will be impossible: "As for us, we cannot help speaking about what we have seen and heard" (Acts 4:20).

Ask Jesus for the same courage and joy.

DAY 4:
THE POETRY OF FAITHFUL WITNESS
Week 8: WHAT IS A WITNESS?

The Bible is full of performance art: from Hosea marrying a prostitute and Ezekiel cooking his food over cow dung, to the parables and miracles of Jesus. The message all the way through is that God uses the imagination. God wants to be understood and embraced by that human faculty as much as any other. Maybe even more.

That could explain why about a third of the Bible (psalms, prophets, and wisdom literature) is poetry of testimony about what individuals have experienced with God, what they have seen God doing, and what they have heard him saying to his people. God is pretty good at speaking to his people with poetry, and his people are pretty good at returning the favor.

So Chase is in good company when he presents his thoughts and experiences of Jesus to his peers as a spoken-word poem. His performance taps into ancient biblical patterns of the prophet and psalmist. What may seem like innovation on Chase's part is actually a return to the wellsprings of spiritual witness. His performance is also well-suited to our own time, since our culture puts a high value on the arts (music, movies, books, etc.) as a means of understanding and interpreting the world.

Let's look at some biblical poetry that speaks of the kind of transformation Chase goes through from undercover Christian to missional psalmist.

Read the Word 📖

Read these portions out loud with your conversation partner, taking two lines each as you go.

I proclaim your saving acts in the great assembly;
I do not seal my lips, Lord, as you know.
I do not hide your righteousness in my heart;
I speak of your faithfulness and your saving help.
I do not conceal your love and your faithfulness
from the great assembly.
Psalm 40:9-10

My people, hear my teaching;
listen to the words of my mouth.
I will open my mouth with a parable;
I will utter hidden things, things from of old—
things we have heard and known,
things our ancestors have told us.
We will not hide them from their descendants;
we will tell the next generation
the praiseworthy deeds of the LORD,
his power, and the wonders he has done.
Psalm 78:1-4

Talk It Over 💬

- What makes a poem a poem? How do you feel about poetry?

- From an artistic point of view, what would you consider the best two lines of poetry in these verses?

Dream it Up

Have you ever tried your hand at some psalm-style poetry writing? If not, consider this an invitation. You don't have to write it in this book, unless you feel like using the inside of the back cover. Even better, grab yourself a fresh sheet of paper and start writing about what you see, feel, hear, and think right now and about what you want to say to God about all of it.

Don't worry about rhyming.

Spend a few minutes writing together now, then perform a few lines for your conversation partner. Keep working on it through the week, if you like.

Pray It Forward

Jesus, since my heart is yours, let my imagination and my tongue also be yours. Open my mouth to utter hidden things, things from of old: your faithfulness and salvation, your love and your truth, God's power and wonder, for the blessing of my world. Amen.

DAY 5:
HOW GOD REACHES US
Week 8: WHAT IS A WITNESS?

Why did God decide to rely on human messengers to spread the knowledge of him amongst the human family? It seems so. . . inefficient.

Why did God place so much responsibility on people like Chase and OB and Grácia and you and me? Didn't he know we'd mess things up half the time? Wouldn't it have been simpler if he had just revealed himself directly to every single person, one by one, age after age?

If this sounds to you like the clay trying to give advice to the potter (Isaiah 45:9), you are hearing right. We're wiser to accept the terms of existence given us than to speculate how another kind of reality might have been better.
That being said, it's worth asking such questions if we're also going to take the time to try to answer them, in admiration of God's ways. They do have answers—rather beautiful ones.

Remember where this guide started out—with a conversation about how we are made for relationship? Well, the brilliant thing God is accomplishing by having the good news of Jesus Christ travel around the world and through human history in the humble pattern of neighbor to neighbor, family to family, and nation to nation—rather than by the "efficient" and "guaranteed" pattern of God-to-individual—is that we all become bound to one another in grateful relationship as a result. We need each other! God's reliance on human messengers gives us the opportunity to become a large extended family of faith, hope, and love.
Let's take a closer look at a particular example from Scripture.

Read the Word

Now an angel of the Lord said to Philip, "Go south to the road—the desert road—that goes down from Jerusalem to Gaza." So he started out, and on his way he met an Ethiopian eunuch, an important official in charge of all the treasury of the Kandake (which means "queen of the Ethiopians"). This man had gone to Jerusalem to worship, and on his way home was sitting in his chariot reading the Book of Isaiah the prophet. The Spirit told Philip, "Go to that chariot and stay near it."

Then Philip ran up to the chariot and heard the man reading Isaiah the prophet. "Do you understand what you are reading?" Philip asked.

"How can I," he said, "unless someone explains it to me?" So he invited Philip to come up and sit with him.

The two men discuss a passage that points to Jesus, the suffering servant who has now risen from the dead to offer forgiveness and new life to the world.

As they travelled along the road, they came to some water and the eunuch said, "Look, here is water. What can stand in the way of my being baptized?" And he gave orders to stop the chariot. Then both Philip and the eunuch went down into the water and Philip baptized him. When they came up out of the water, the Spirit of the Lord suddenly took Philip away, and the eunuch did not see him again, but went on his way rejoicing. **Acts 8:26–31; 36–39**

Think It Over

The way we roll with God's pattern of spreading the good news is by remaining attentive to God, attentive to others, and ready for anything. We know that God can use anyone for his work, so it's not all up to us. But at the same time, why not us? There is joy in playing our own obedient role in God's master plan for the salvation of the world.

Talk It Over

- Who led you to faith, and what is your relationship with that person now?

- What do you find interesting about the story of Philip and the Ethiopian?

Pray It Forward

Spirit of God, thank you for leading me into faith. Open my eyes to see the people around me, and my ears to hear your voice, so that I might share this faith with others who are looking for it.

CONVERSATION 3

WILL ANYONE LISTEN?

REPRESENTING FAITH TO A HOSTILE WORLD

GROUP SESSION

When Grace is put on the spot in debate class, she rises to the occasion and gives an assertive but respectful explanation of what she believes about the origin of the universe. Mr. Brady is somehow able to disagree with his colleague Mr. Livingston on matters of profound belief but still be his good friend. How do these people pull this off? What's their secret? In this session, we try to find out.

 **REEL to REAL**

1. **Grace debates Mr. Livingston**

- What are some words that describe Grace's style in this debate?

- When Chase presents his poem to the class, we see that there is a place for personal experience in making an appeal for faith. Is there also a place for reason and logic, as Grace demonstrates?

- Which position do you think takes more faith: to believe in God or to be an atheist?

- What are some words to describe Mr. Livingston's style? Why does he get so emotionally involved? What specific things does Grace say that upset him?

- Why does the question of God and cosmic origins become personal for people?

- Would you say that an anti-God or anti-Christian bias exists in most schools? In your school, do you feel free to share your convictions without fear?

- Would a pro-Christian bias be fair? If not, what might be a fair middle ground?

2. Friends with different beliefs

- How does Mr. Livingston feel about the debate with Grace after it's over?

- How would you describe the friendship between Mr. Brady and Mr. Livingston? Give specific examples.

- Have you ever had a friendship like this, in which you were clear about your own identity and had "agreed to disagree" with someone else? What's good about these kinds of friendships?

- As a teacher, is Mr. Brady free to communicate his convictions at school? Should he be?

ENGAGE THE WORD

Today's passage is from Acts 17:16–34.

- What is Paul's opening line in his conversation at the Areopagus? What is its purpose?

- Can you see any other examples of Paul trying to establish common ground with the Athenians?

- What is the main thing he is trying to communicate to them?

- Why do some of the Athenians sneer in verse 32? Was belief in resurrection from the dead a problem even for people in the ancient world? (Take a look at Mark 12:18 and following for another example.)

- How did Paul know when to stop?

- Do you see any similarities between Paul and Grace? Any differences, other than age and gender?

- What are some ways young people in our time can put into practice Paul's approach to representing the faith?

CARRY IT OUT
Tag-team Debate Role-plays

In your small groups, improvise debates in teams of 2 on a topic listed below. Only one person on a team can speak at a time. Whenever you're ready to switch turns, tag hands with your partner.

Flip a coin to decide which pair takes which side of the argument. Use the following yes-or-no topics:

- Jesus's disciples must have faked his resurrection
- All religions lead to the same God
- Christians are mean and intolerant
- Christians should confine their faith to their private lives
- Prayer doesn't make sense
- There's too much evil in the world for there to be a good God

Follow rules of good argument: Don't attack the person. Keep things warm and respectful. As you focus on the ideas under debate, don't forget about the value of the person sitting in front of you, even though you disagree.

DAY 1:
AS SHREWD AS SNAKES
Week 9: WILL ANYONE LISTEN?

In the cafeteria after Grácia's debate with Mr. Livingston, Chase and OB express their astonishment at what she has just accomplished. Her confidence, intelligence, and general demeanor have inspired them that it is possible to hold your head up as a Christian in a tense situation and give logical, compelling reasons for being a person of faith.

As we consider such debating activity more closely this week, we want to begin with a look at our best model as Christians: the Lord we follow.

Jesus was familiar with public conversation and controversy. Most of his ministry consisted of walking around interacting with groups of people in public spaces. Some of those people pushed back in debate every now and then, especially as the state of affairs intensified during that final Passover week in Jerusalem. Debate sometimes revolved around Jesus's action, sometimes around his words, and often around both. Since the common people were so impressed with him, the leaders who were envious of Jesus did everything they could to make him seem in the wrong. But he was more than their match.

Read the Word

Jesus entered the temple courts, and, while he was teaching, the chief priests and the elders of the people came to him. "By what authority are you doing these things?" they asked. "And who gave you this authority?"

Jesus replied, "I will also ask you one question. If you answer me, I will tell you by what authority I am doing these things. John's baptism—where did it come from? Was it from heaven, or of human origin?"

They discussed it among themselves and said, "If we say, 'From heaven,' he will ask, 'Then why didn't you believe him?' But if we say, 'Of human origin'—we are afraid of the people, for they all hold that John was a prophet."

So they answered Jesus, "We don't know."
Matthew 21:23–27

Then the Pharisees went out and laid plans to trap him in his words. They sent their disciples to him along with the Herodians. "Teacher," they said, "we know that you are a man of integrity and that you teach the way of God in accordance with the truth. You aren't swayed by others, because you pay no attention to who they are. Tell us then, what is your opinion? Is it right to pay the imperial tax to Caesar or not?"

But Jesus, knowing their evil intent, said, "You hypocrites, why are you trying to trap me? Show me the coin used for paying the tax." They brought him a denarius, and he asked them, "Whose image is this? And whose inscription?"

"Caesar's," they replied.

Then he said to them, "So give back to Caesar what is Caesar's, and to God what is God's."

When they heard this, they were amazed. So they left him and went away.
Matthew 22:15–22

If Jesus had answered either yes or no to the Pharisees' question about the imperial tax, he would've been saying something treasonous either in the eyes of the Roman authorities or in the eyes of his Rome-oppressed Jewish compatriots. Their question was a calculated trap. But he navigated the issue with finesse, lifting it above the contentious "for-or-against" of worldly special interest and forcing people to consider the state of their own hearts before God.

Group after group took on Jesus that day. It finally ended when he put the ball back in his opponents' court so effectively that "No one could say a word in reply, and from that day on no one dared to ask him any more questions" (Matthew 22:46).

Think It Over

Mark's version of that day includes the comment, "The large crowd listened to him with delight" (Mark 12:37). People love it when the usual authorities are shown up by a rookie. We see that happen in Grácia's debate class, as the students start expressing their support for her against Mr. Livingston.

But this kind of thing can also get dangerous for a newcomer. Authorities don't like to be shown up. In Jesus's case it led to his death. In Grácia's case, Mr. Livingston comes to his senses in the staff room. But one other envious person in the classroom hatches her own plot to strike back at both Grácia and a teacher she and Chase cherish.

Talk It Over

- One of the important skills Jesus demonstrates in these stories is knowing how not to get trapped by someone else's malicious question. Has anyone ever tried to trap you in this way? What did you say?

- Later on, when Jesus is put on trial by the authorities, there are times he even says nothing at all in response to people's verbal attacks. He just remains silent and lets them listen to their own words (Mark 14:61). What is the effect of doing that?

Dream it Up 🎨

Imagine that Jesus was carrying on his earthly ministry in our own time. What kind of hot-button issue might his opponents use to try to trap him? Imagine a short scene and write it up for your conversation partner.

Pray It Forward 🙏

We aren't expected to be as sharp-witted in debate as Jesus was. He was Jesus, after all—the very wisdom of God.

At the same time, Jesus expresses his character and gifts in his followers. He gave us an interesting command to guide us on our way: "I am sending you out like sheep among wolves. Therefore be as shrewd as snakes and as innocent as doves" (Matthew 10:16).

Ask Jesus to give you that gift.

DAY 2:
AS INNOCENT AS DOVES
Week 9: WILL ANYONE LISTEN?

Today let's look at the other half of Jesus's command—the "dove" part.

While Grácia demonstrates shrewdness in debating Mr. Livingston, she also demonstrates a quality of innocence. Even as her teacher gets hot under the collar, she never departs from her basic stance of respect. She is able to be assertive without being insulting.

"No disrespect, Mr. Livingston, but from where I'm standing, it seems like your position would take more faith than mine," she says. And later, "Mr. Livingston, it feels like every time I speak about creation in this way at school, I'm either shut down, laughed at, or both. What about open-minded dialogue? What about the pursuit of truth?"

Such respectfulness is one more reason that her classmates temporarily abandon their enthusiasm for Darwinism and start cheering her on, proud to see one of their own number conduct herself with such poise in argument.

Read the Word

We've got some helpful biblical guidance on this subject of respect—words written to New Testament disciples who faced much opposition, some of it violent, in those early years of the church.

Do not repay evil with evil or insult with insult. On the contrary, repay evil with blessing, because to this you were called so that you may inherit a blessing. . .

Always be prepared to give an answer to everyone who asks you to give the reason for the hope that you have. But do this with gentleness and respect, keeping a clear conscience, so that those who speak maliciously against your good behavior in Christ may be ashamed of their slander.
1 Peter 3:9, 15–16

Don't have anything to do with foolish and stupid arguments, because you know they produce quarrels. And the Lord's servant must not be quarrelsome but must be kind to everyone, able to teach, not resentful. Opponents must be gently instructed, in the hope that God will grant them repentance leading them to a knowledge of the truth.
2 Timothy 2:23–25

In the preceding passage, Paul is advising Timothy as much about debate within the church as outside it—but the same principles hold. In any situation, the way we speak says as much to an opponent as *what* we say. Since that fundamental message, for a Christian, is the good news that God's love is saving the world in Jesus, it's necessary that we communicate with kindness and with truth.

Think It Over

"Winning the argument" isn't the goal of Christian debate as much as "winning the person." Sometimes the second goal may be better served by losing the argument—not intentionally but as a consequence of holding love as more important than proving yourself right and someone else wrong. The cross looked like a lost argument to Jesus's world, but it unleashed a power of redemption that wouldn't have been found if Jesus had come down and started knocking heads together in answer to his enemies' taunts.

In Grácia's case, it appears that she does win the argument. The goal of the "dove" in a situation like this is to protect the dignity of the one who lost. That's why Grácia nips in the bud Jorge's plan to post a video of the debate on YouTube immediately after class. "You can't make a mockery of Mr. Livingston," she says. "He's a good and decent man."

Talk It Over

- How would you rate the proportion of shrewdness-to-innocence in Grace's character? What would you say is the ideal Christian proportion?

- When was the last time you lost or won an argument? Is there anything you could have done differently in either argument, in honor of the reality of God's saving love?

Try It Out ✔

Next time you're in an argument with a member of your family, try losing in love, just to know what it feels like.

- If someone asked you to explain the reason for your Christian hope, what would your answer be? Try writing one here, on the spot.

Pray It Forward 🙏

Lord, teach me to bless those who curse me. Give me your own Spirit, that I may trust the resurrection power that overturns the shame of the cross.

DAY 3:
LIVE SUCH GOOD LIVES
Week 9: WILL ANYONE LISTEN?

"Preach the gospel at all times. When necessary, use words." Saint Francis of Assisi is credited with this wry counsel on Christian evangelism. He was suggesting that our lives have the greatest communicative power of all. Therefore we should shape our actions to illustrate the gospel—that is, the good news that God loves us, that God has come  to be with us, that God forgives and heals us, that God is reigning in this world, and that a reconciled relationship with him is possible in Christ.

Can you think of anyone in *Because of Grácia* whose life might say that kind of thing?

How about Mr. Brady? As a schoolteacher, there are limits on what he can explain about his beliefs, unless asked directly. Even on the neutral ground of the school staff room, Mr. Brady exercises a degree of caution—not exactly the ashamed "hiding" of Chase, but the watchful restraint of someone wanting to keep his place at the table in a secular work environment. That being said, Mr. Brady definitely seems free to live as a Christian in his personality, "preaching the gospel at all times" through his friendship with Mr. Livingston. That colleague's respect for him—and eventual defense of him—is a testimony to what Mr. Brady is communicating.

Grace's relationship with Bobbi follows a similar pattern. And at a crucial moment, "when necessary," Grace certainly does use words.

These characters follow an ideal established by Scripture. The rock of the church, Peter, has some more great things to say on the subject.

Read the Word

Dear friends, I urge you, as foreigners and exiles, to abstain from sinful desires, which wage war against your soul. Live such good lives among the pagans that, though they accuse you of doing wrong, they may see your good deeds and glorify God on the day he visits us. . .

For it is God's will that by doing good you should silence the ignorant talk of foolish people.
1 Peter 2:11–12; 15

Peter learned this kind of thing from his master, Jesus, whose words we read a couple weeks ago:

Let your light shine before others, that they may see your good deeds and glorify your Father in heaven.
Matthew 5:16

In a roundabout way, Mr. Livingston glorifies God in the principal's office when he sticks up for his friend. "You know I don't believe in God," he says to Principal Schwab, "but it's the biggest part of who Brady is and I respect him for it. It's the reason he's able to reach so many of his students." Mr. L has taken note of Mr. B's shining light over the years.

Talk It Over 💬

- Was Saint Francis saying that we never need to talk about the gospel? If not, how do we know when it's time to talk?

- Is there a context in your life in which any "preaching of the gospel" that you might do has to take place through actions alone? Has anyone ever shown the gospel to you without using words?

Ask A Mentor ❓

Ask your usual mentor how much freedom they have to speak about their faith in their workplace. Can they share any stories of the effect "good deeds" have had on other people's attitudes to God?

Pray It Forward 🙏

In the form of a prayer, tell God what you would like your life to communicate to others.

DAY 4:
I WILL GIVE YOU WORDS
Week 9: WILL ANYONE LISTEN?

"Grace, how do you know all that stuff?" Jorge asks in disbelief during the origins-of-life debate.

"My dad—he talks about it all the time."

"Seriously?"

The intellectual climate of Grace's home has provided an ongoing preparation for her to be able to give an answer to anyone who asks the reason for the hope she has (1 Peter 3:15).

Chase asks her a further question in the lunchroom later on: "How did you know all that stuff about Mr. Livingston?"

Grace says she just looked at the pictures on his wall, noticed a certain progression, and made a guess about the direction in which Mr. L's worldview might be developing.

In a real-life version of this story, we would have to suspect the Holy Spirit's involvement in someone discovering such a timely insight right when it was needed. There are promises in Scripture about the Spirit giving us just this kind of help-on-the-fly. Such promises are crucial for us to know and trust, so that even in our preparing ahead of time to give an answer for the hope we have, we never start believing it all comes down to our own skill in generating the right words. The Bible makes it clear that the right words come from God.

Read the Word

As usual, take turns speaking the Word to one another.

"On my account you will be brought before governors and kings as witnesses to them and to the Gentiles. But when they arrest you, do not worry about what to say or how to say it. At that time you will be given what to say, for it will not be you speaking, but the Spirit of your Father speaking through you."
Matthew 10:18–20

"When you are brought before synagogues, rulers, and authorities, do not worry about how you will defend yourselves or what you will say, for the Holy Spirit will teach you at that time what you should say."
Luke 12:11–12

"Make up your mind not to worry beforehand how you will defend yourselves. For I will give you words and wisdom that none of your adversaries will be able to resist or contradict."
Luke 21:14–15

Now Stephen, a man full of God's grace and power, performed great wonders and signs among the people. Opposition arose, however, from members of the Synagogue of the Freedmen . . . [These men] began to argue with Stephen. But they could not stand up against the wisdom the Spirit gave him as he spoke.
Act 6:8–10

These examples show the Holy Spirit guiding speech in situations of conflict and crisis. That isn't the only time he guides us, though. The Bible often shows the Spirit taking the lead to generate an affirmative word of witness to the world, as he does at Pentecost. That's the name of the Jewish festival the early Christians were celebrating when the Spirit came upon them with power, as promised by Jesus. On that day, he kindled a wild declaration of the wonders of God in every language possible.

In trying to explain to the onlookers what was going on, the former fisherman Peter preached a Spirit-inspired sermon that resulted in the repentance and baptism of 3,000 people.

Pray It Forward 🙏

Paul wrote this at the conclusion of Ephesians: "Pray also for me, that whenever I speak, words may be given me so that I will fearlessly make known the mystery of the gospel" (6:19).

Pray the same thing for yourself.

Talk It Over 💬

• Have you ever had an experience of God helping you find just the right words to say?

• How does a person get good at hearing the Holy Spirit?

• Do the words of Jesus you read today encourage you or make you nervous? Explain.

DAY 5:
THE LIGHT OF GOD'S FACE
Week 9: WILL ANYONE LISTEN?

The Holy Spirit doesn't stop at giving us the right words to say. What if those good words simply went out into the world, fell to the ground, and were trampled underfoot? What if the people to whom they were directed were "ever seeing but never perceiving, and ever hearing but never understanding" (Mark 4:12)?

No, the Holy Spirit doesn't stop at the right words. He also prepares minds and hearts out there in the world to receive them. He works in us, but he also works in others. That's so important, because the world in which we speak words of God can be a pretty dry and rocky place.

Read the Word 📖

Psalm 4 puts it this way:

Many are saying, "Who will show us any good?" Lift up the light of Your countenance upon us, O Lord!
Psalm 4:6 nasb

"Who will show us any good?" There are faces in the background of Chase and Grace's school classroom, and our own classrooms, that seem to make the same challenge. "Who can persuade us that God is worth believing in? Who can convince us that life is worth living?" That can be a hard attitude for a believer in God to face day after day. Psalm 42 agrees:

My tears have been my food day and night, while people say to me all day long, "Where is your God?" . . . My bones suffer mortal agony as my foes taunt me, saying to me all day long, "Where is your God?"
Psalm 42:3, 10

Grace's version of this lament can be heard in her heartfelt reply to Mr. Livingston's materialistic view of the universe: "Don't you find that depressing?"

Think It Over

Indeed, it would be depressing to live in a world where every emotion could be traced back to chemical urges, every decision linked to some biological necessity in an enormous web of cause and effect. It would be dismal if every meaningful human activity—including music, worship, art, poetry, laughter, family, beauty, joy, and love itself—could be boiled to down to just one more variation on the brute law of nature. When people believe this way, what can be done for them? Who can show them any good?

At the end of the day, we must come back to a confident trust that the same God who could make himself known to us can also make himself known to others. He can lift up the light of his countenance—he can shine the light of his face upon them. God has a loving power to do that, which goes far beyond anything we could ever communicate ourselves.

Talk It Over

- Do you ever feel depressed or discouraged about people's indifference to God?

- Which group do you think has more people in it: a) those who want to believe in God but can't bring themselves to do so; or b) those who don't want to believe in God and therefore suppress their suspicion that he might exist?

- Acts 16:34 talks about a jailer who was "filled with joy because he had come to believe in God." Who is someone in your life right now that you would love to have the same experience as that jailer?

Try It Out ✔

Post your meme on Facebook or some other public forum. See if anyone asks you what it's about. Perhaps the friend you named in the last Talk It Over question will ask you about it. See if you find yourself with an opportunity to have a Holy Spirit–guided conversation.

MEME-orize It

Find or create an appropriate image to caption with the words, "Many are saying, 'Who will show us any good?'" Share it with your conversation partner.

Pray It Forward

Let the light of your face shine upon us, O Lord.
Let the light of your face shine upon us.

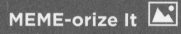

ABOUT THE AUTHORS

CHRIS FRIESEN

A teacher and pastor by profession and a songwriter and storyteller on the side, Chris Friesen holds a master's degree in theology from Mennonite Brethren Biblical Seminary at Fresno Pacific University and has worked for years in youth, young adult, and children's ministry, from the Canadian boreal forest to the inner city. He resides in Saskatoon, Saskatchewan, on the Canadian prairies, where he makes music with his wife and six children in the Friesen Family Band.

MICHELLE SIMES

Michelle Simes is a Special Education teacher and homeschool mom who is married to Tom, the writer/ director of *Because Of Grácia*. She has written pro-life and youth curriculum material for schools and churches. Michelle has worked in ministry to teens and young adults around the areas of chastity and sanctity of life issues. She currently resides in the heartland of Canada, Saskatoon, Saskatchewan. Michelle and Tom have been blessed with 33 years of marriage and four beautiful children ages 16-26.

BECAUSE of GRÁCIA

PRODUCTS AND RESOURCES

BECAUSE OF GRÁCIA: A Novel

Based on the award-winning film.

ISBN: 978-1-947297-00-5
eBook: 978-1-947297-01-2

Abbreviated leader's guides for teaching individual themes

A Film and Faith Leader Guide: Theme 1 Practicing Friendship

ISBN: 978-1-947297-06-7
eBook: 978-1-947297-07-4

BECAUSE OF GRÁCIA: Leader Guide
A Film and Faith Conversation Guide

Leader's companion to guide students through curriculum.

ISBN: 978-1-947297-04-3
eBook: 978-1-947297-05-0

A Film and Faith Leader Guide: Theme 2 Choosing Life

ISBN: 978-1-947297-08-1
eBook: 978-1-947297-09-8

A Film and Faith Leader Guide: Theme 3 Voicing Faith

ISBN: 978-1-947297-10-4
eBook: 978-1-947297-11-1

BECAUSE OF GRÁCIA: Curriculum Bundle

Includes the leader's guide, one student guide and DVD clips from the film.

ISBN: 978-1-947297-12-8

AVAILABLE WHEREVER BOOKS ARE SOLD

For ordering information, visit **dexteritycollective.co** or write to **info@dexteritycollective.co**.